THE SACRED ART OF SELF-DESTRUCTION

AWAKENING

THE SACRED SERIES
BOOK 2

SHADOW EASTON

LUCAS EASTON

Copyright © 2025 by Katana Publishing LLC, Sacramento, CA

All rights reserved.

No part of this book may be reproduced in any form or by any electronic or mechanical means, including information storage and retrieval systems, without written permission from the author, except for the use of brief quotations in a book review.

NO AI TRAINING: Without in any way limiting the author's [and publisher's] exclusive rights under copyright, any use of this Publication and its contents to "train" generative artificial intelligence (AI) technologies to generate text or Frameworks is expressly prohibited. The author reserves all rights to license uses of this work for generative AI training and the development of machine learning language models.

Print ISBN: 979-8-9906182-3-7

E-Book ISBN: 979-8-9906182-5-1

DISCLAIMER

Our society has a belief in sickness. As such, we have the medical industrial complex as well as battalions of attorneys that work to ensure that the medical establishment is believed to be the only authority on the subject of health and sickness. To comply with their requirements, we must include the following.

The Authors provide the Book, information, content, and/or data (collectively, "Information") contained therein for informational purposes only. The Authors do not provide any medical advice in the Book, and the Information should not be so construed or used. Nothing contained in the Book is intended to create a physician-patient relationship, to replace the services of a licensed, trained physician or health professional, or to be a substitute for medical advice from a physician or trained health professional licensed in your state. Do not rely on anything contained in the Book, and consult a physician licensed in your state in all matters relating to your health. You hereby agree that you shall not make any health or medical-related decision based in whole or in part on anything contained in the Book.

This book is not therapy.

It is not medical advice. It is not a spiritual path, practice, or method.

It does not promise healing, peace, freedom, or a better version of you.

What follows is demolition. The structures that collapse under Lenswork include the ones you may still believe you need: your history, your purpose, your sense of control, even the "you" who thinks it can survive this process.

If you are seeking comfort, affirmation, or a system of beliefs to adopt, stop here. If you are under medical or psychiatric care, continue only with the awareness that this text is not a substitute for that.

Nothing in these pages belongs to anyone.

Nothing here can be possessed, protected, or practiced.

Lenswork dissolves scaffolding. What remains may not be survivable by the identity reading this line. Proceed knowing there is no guarantee of reward, only the exposure of what has always been false.

The Authors are not responsible for the reader's emotional or physical reactions to anything in this book, including but not limited to: Anxiety, Anger, Heart Palpitations, Emotional Pain or Suffering, Spiritual Psychosis, Identity Crisis, Depression, Loss of Appetite, Digestive Issues, Blood Pressure Readings, Paranoia, Sudden Onset Critical Thinking, Psychosis of any kind, Mood Disorders, Feelings of Bliss, Truth-Realization, Mystical Experiences of any kind, Ear Ringing, Body Aches, Symptoms of any kind, Alien Abduction, U.T.I's, Hormone levels, Allergic reactions of any kind, and physical and/or emotional issues of any kind.

Neither the authors nor the publisher assumes any responsibility for errors, omissions, or contrary interpretations of the subject matter herein. Any perceived slight of any individual or organization is purely unintentional and is not to be considered hate speech of any kind. Brand and product names are trademarks or registered trademarks of their respective owners.

PREFACE
WHEN THE EGO READS THIS, IT WILL TRY TO STEAL IT

Our first book, *Spiritual Nonsense – The Sacred Art of SELF-Deception,* was satire. We wrote it as a mirror held up to the Spiritual Industrial Complex, a place where incense, affirmations, and "higher truths" are sold like trinkets in a market. That book mocked the costumes, exposed the absurdity, and invited readers to begin questioning the trade itself.

This book is different.

Mockery can only take you so far. The problem runs deeper than the clowns selling spirituality. The problem is structural, which means the words themselves—"awakening," "enlightenment," "truth," "freedom"—are already corrupted. They carry centuries of misuse, abuse, and product packaging. Use them as they are, and the reader's mind instantly fills in the old grooves of meaning.

So here, we don't play that game. We had to create a new language. Words with precise definitions. Words you will not find in the marketplace. Words invented to keep you from dragging old assumptions into new terrain. You may notice Fracture Point, Rupture, Collapse, Lenswork. These are not poetic flourishes; they

PREFACE

are tools. They exist because nothing in the existing vocabulary could hold the solvent without leaking illusion back into it.

And this book had to be written in a way the ego cannot easily hijack. Every system, every teaching, every method becomes another badge the ego wears.

This book is not a badge. Its form, its rhythm, its interruptions—all of it was designed to prevent the reader from turning the solvent into a possession.

If at times the style feels strange, abrasive, or even hostile, that is not an accident. It is protection.

If the first book made fun of the costumes, this one burns down the stage.

CONTENTS

Before We Begin	xiii
The Repair Loop *The Man Who Couldn't Stop Patching the Cage*	1
Fake Awake *Ambien Sleepwalkers Selling You a Dream of Awakening*	73
The Great Distortion *Everything You Think You See Is Backwards*	79
The Myth of the Separate Self *The Most Expensive Lie You Ever Bought*	83
Ego Architecture *Meet the Warden of Your Invisible Prison*	87
Simulation Explained *The Code That Writes "You" in Real Time*	95
The Trap of Language *How Words Build the Cage You Live In*	115
The Body-Mind Hoax *The Fake Divorce That Keeps You Chasing*	123
SELF-Help Trap *When the Solution Is Just a Better-Branded Problem*	143
The Healing Simulation *When the Cure Becomes Part of the Disease*	155
Spirituality, Spiritual Authority, and the Guru Illusion *How the Ego Hides in Holy Clothing*	163
The Truth Illusion *Why Chasing Reality Keeps You Asleep*	175
Awakening, Enlightenment, Collapse *Words That Have Lied to You*	185
Fracture Point *When the Game You Trusted Starts to Rot*	187
Rupture: What It Is and What It Is Not *The Break the Structure Rushes to Repair*	195
The Witness Trap *The Final Costume Change of "Me"*	205
Collapse Is Not a Crisis *When the Bottom Falls Out and Nothing Breaks*	223

The Quiet after Collapse *Life With No One Left to Live It*	231
Lenswork *The Structural Dissolution of All Claims*	241
Workbook / The Sacred Work of SELF-Destruction *Life With No One Left to Live It*	273
The End of the Map *When There's Nowhere Left to Go*	281
Bonus Chapter: Lenswork in the Wild *No Exceptions. No Survivors*	285
Closing Strike *Nowhere Left to Stand*	313
Bonus Material: The Mechanics of the Illusion *The Machine That Runs Without a Driver*	315
Glossary of Collapse	325

BEFORE WE BEGIN
WHAT THIS IS, AND WHY IT DOESN'T BELONG TO ANYONE

What you're holding is not a teaching. It's not a philosophy, a worldview, a theory, or a belief system.

It's not ours. It's not yours. It's not anyone's.

What follows is **Lenswork,** a way of looking that, once applied, dissolves every structure that depends on the existence of a "you."

It's not "knowledge" in the sense the Self can collect and store. And once it's applied, it doesn't stop at the bits you don't like. It strips everything, the inspiring parts, the comforting parts, the impressive parts, until nothing remains for identity to hang on.

Lenswork isn't an imported framework, teaching, philosophy, or belief that comes from any external authority. It's not handed down from a guru, tradition, or school of thought. It's what shows itself when the usual filters drop.

It can't be "given" to you, and it can't be owned. It's either seen or not seen. If that sounds extreme, **good.**

This is not a gentle sanding of rough edges. **It's demolition.**

BEFORE WE BEGIN

Where It Comes From (Spoiler: Nowhere)

Lenswork doesn't come from a guru, a sacred text, or an exotic mountain cave.

It emerges naturally when you look at reality without using the filters of:

Ego
Identity
Comfort
Cultural or Spiritual Bias

When those filters are gone, what's left is structural clarity, and life behaves exactly like a simulation.

Not a machine, not a computer, but as total appearance rendered through perception, conditioning, and the language of a fictional Self.

Lenswork is like solvent. It doesn't leave room for ambiguity or lingering illusions. Once applied, it dissolves every construct within the simulation by revealing that all of them, from your most personal memories to your loftiest spiritual ideals, are part of the same dualistic game.

Some dissolutions are partial, Ruptures that damage the Self's machinery but leave it capable of repair. Collapse is different: the Self's machinery is gone, and with it, the operator.

Seen this way, everything inside the simulation can be explained with absolute clarity. Not because it gains a new meaning, but because its basis is exposed. Lenswork "destroys" everything, not by smashing it in chaos, but by showing that none of it was ever solid to begin with.

BEFORE WE BEGIN

Why Call It a "Simulation"?

Because when you examine life through Lenswork, it behaves like one:

The "World" you know is always filtered through a model of it.

Identity is a character role inside that model, not a fact.

Everything, from memory to meaning, is a set piece that can disappear if the role disappears.

> The word "simulation" is not a metaphysical claim.
> **It's a working description, a functional lens.**

Lenswork is a tool of complete clarity inside the simulation. It explains everything by showing that everything is just part of that simulation.

And once seen, the whole illusion becomes transparent.

It's what you call reality when you've stripped away every comforting lie the Ego tells to keep itself alive.

The Mechanics - The Five Pillars of Simulation

What we call "reality" is a sustained projection. Its stability depends on a set of reinforcing assumptions:

• **Separation**: The unquestioned division between "Self" and "not-Self." Without it, there's no subject to experience objects.

• **Continuity**: The sense that this "Self" persists over time. Past and future bind together to form the story of "me."

• **Narrative**: Events are chained into cause-and-effect sequences, creating the illusion of meaning and progression.

- **Ownership:** Experiences are claimed as "mine" and "yours," anchoring identity into every perception.
- **Meaning**: Value judgments (good/bad, success/failure) feed the drama loop, ensuring the story matters to the one inside it.

Remove one of these, and the simulation wobbles. Remove all of them, and it Collapses.

> Illusion isn't a haze over reality; it is the structure reality appears as.

Why You Can Trust This (Without Believing It)

You don't need to believe any of this. Belief is just another structure inside the simulation.

What you can do is apply Lenswork and see what it does.

If it's just a nice idea, nothing happens. If it's structurally sound, the scaffolding of the "Self" will start to buckle on its own.

That's the only test that matters here.

Before We Get Going, A Quick Word Map

You'll run into certain terms in this book.

Here's the shorthand so you're not left wondering until later:

Simulation: The structural illusion of reality (total field of appearance) as filtered through identity.

Character: The fictional role (EGO Character) playing inside the simulation.

Ego: The maintenance system (EGO Structure) that keeps the character feeling real.

Collapse: The permanent dismantling of the Ego-character structure, leaving no center from which a "Self" can operate. This is irreversible. No Self remains to process, interpret, or report it.

Rupture: A fracture in the identity structure where its normal functioning breaks. This can range from small cracks to near-total shutdown. Unlike Collapse, Rupture can heal, rebuild, or adapt. All so-called "awakenings" are Ruptures, the Self survives, only altered.

Fracture Point: The moment the story starts coming apart, but the set is still standing.

Lenswork: The act of applying this seeing, stripping away every Ego-dependent structure until only clarity remains.

You don't have to memorize any of this now.

By the time we're done, you won't just "understand" these terms; you'll have watched them dismantle everything they describe.

The No Reward Clause

This is not a path to something better. There is nothing to gain and no one to gain it.

If you approach Lenswork as a way to become freer, happier, more peaceful, or more "enlightened," you've already left the territory. That's just the Ego switching masks, from ordinary Self to "Spiritual Self."

Collapse doesn't deliver a prize. It doesn't leave you as a perfected version of yourself. It leaves no you at all.

If that sounds bleak, it's because the one reading this is built on the hope of reward. Without that hope, there's no reason for it to continue, which is precisely the point.

This is not the highest rung of the ladder. This is the removal of the ladder and the one who would climb it.

❦ At The Bar:

You: "So this… Lenswork… is your philosophy?"

Me: "If it was a philosophy, you could agree with it and keep your Self intact. This isn't about agreement; it's about stripping the Self until there's nothing left to agree."

You: "Sounds like a belief system with better branding."

Me: "Belief is what you cling to when you don't actually see. This is for when you're ready to burn the scaffolding, not decorate it."

You: "Okay… but where did you get it?"

Me: "Nowhere. It's what's left when you stop importing other people's truths and actually look. Doesn't belong to anyone, not even the one speaking right now."

You: "And you're sure it works?"

Me: "It's not medicine. It's acid. You don't 'trust' acid; you drop it on something and watch what disappears."

THE REPAIR LOOP
THE MAN WHO COULDN'T STOP PATCHING THE CAGE

The following story is true. Though the names have been changed, Mike is a real person and these events unfolded. This retelling is from Shadow's recollection and journal entries she wrote during this timeframe. We'll be looking at the story to clearly see the Ego mechanics in addiction, recovery, reshaping, Fracture Point, and Rupture. The rest of the book will break down the Ego structure, Ego character, and the simulation in detail. We'll be referring to this story in those examples. It's a heck of a tale. Buckle up.

Lucas and I have known Mike for over 20 years. He's funny, extroverted, quick with a laugh, and very charming. He doesn't know a stranger; he has that amazing ability to simply talk to anyone and walk away with a new 'mate,' as he would call them. He's from the UK, so the accent really plays well here in the United States. Mike is quite tall, about 6'3", and most would find him handsome.

He has dark, closely cropped hair, brown eyes hidden behind stylish glasses, and keeps his beard in that five o'clock shadow style most of the time. He has a full arm sleeve tattoo that he got a few years ago, wears heavy silver bracelets, a chunky silver chain necklace, and a pinky ring that looks like one of those Celtic knots.

His look, on first glance is a little edgy, but the ready smile and sincere friendliness take that edge off.

Mike has a wife, Naomi, and two sons, Alex and Andrew. I say 'he has a wife' rather than 'he's married' because the relationship was already dead when they married. They hadn't known one another long, and she got pregnant, so naturally, they got married and stayed married 'for the kids.' They've been married for 23 years.

I've never met Naomi, and Lucas hasn't seen her in many years. We've both spent a little time with Alex and Andrew here and there over the years, but our long-term friendship was with Mike.

Mike and Naomi lived in a cute house in a quaint neighborhood. It's small but charming, with a detached garage at the back of the house and a fairly large yard filled with flowers and a gazebo hung with solar lights, making it a lovely spot for dinner in the evening. I was only in the house once. It was decorated in a shabby chic style that could have been cozy, but it had no warmth.

The house simply felt cold, like there was no life in it. The life it did have was found in the two little mixed-breed dogs that they all absolutely adored. The dogs, as much as anything, may have been the one binding tie that they had in common.

Their marriage isn't a relationship so much as simply an obligation that neither Mike nor Naomi have the energy to do anything about. For many years, it was a friendly, if loveless arrangement and it worked for a time.

The arrangement began to wear thin, especially as the boys grew up and the parenting responsibilities changed. By the time the boys were teenagers, there wasn't really anything holding the 'relationship' together any longer.

Mike was increasingly unhappy. He didn't leave, though; he simply renovated the garage and made that his room. Naomi and the boys had the house; Mike had his room, and their lives continued to drift apart all the while maintaining the illusion of a happy family to the outside world.

We've had many conversations with Mike over the years, trying to understand why he would stay in a situation that he was clearly miserable in, but all he could ever say was he didn't want to hurt his boys. Never realizing that the boys were already affected by the complete lie their home life was.

Mike ran a small business that was very customer-oriented. He had quite a few high-profile people as clients, and they loved both his work and the service he provided. Mike's character really lent itself to customer interaction. He made everyone feel heard and taken care of. His pricing was fair, often below market rate because he enjoyed helping people, until that too began to wear thin.

One evening, Mike shared with us that he hated his business. This was a surprise to us. He said he kind of just fell into it, that there was no passion for the work and it had only been a suggested opportunity.

As Mike told it, "The business wasn't even my idea; it was the idea of a client that I was doing work for. He said he would fund the start-up costs. I didn't know what else to do, so I agreed. Next thing I know, a week before the funding was to arrive, the client had a heart attack and died. I was so lost; I still didn't know what else to do, so I used my credit cards to get going and went ahead and opened. There was no real thought-out intention; it just kind of happened."

Our friend was now unhappy at home and unhappy at work but had no idea what to do about either situation. He felt stuck in both.

Little by little, Mike began to go off the rails. He was always a drinker, but generally just on weekends or social occasions. With everything in his life falling apart, drinking slowly began to take him over—harder liquor and more frequent—until it came to the point that he was starting his day with a glass of vodka with a splash of coke.

He began drinking all day, every day, little sips here and there through the morning, and then about three in the afternoon, he really poured it on. His story about this behavior was that he was so unhappy at home that he needed to be three sheets to the wind to even walk into the house. Then a bottle of wine with dinner and maybe another few nightcaps until he passed out in his cozy garage room.

He would often tell us, "My family doesn't even acknowledge me when I come home from work. Sometimes, Andrew cooks dinner, but most nights it's everyone for themselves. The boys stay in their rooms, and Naomi sits in the living room watching TV. It's like I'm not even there."

He would go on to say, "It makes me so angry that I work so hard, at a business I don't even like, mind you, to provide for them. I pay for everything: the house, cars to drive, clothes to wear, food to eat, and they can't even be bothered to say, 'Hi, how was your day?'"

To the outside world, he hid this spiral pretty well. It may be that his family were the only ones who noticed, *if* they noticed. His business was still running, bills were still paid, and the family was taken care of. When we saw him for the occasional dinner, it was clear to us that he had already had a few when he arrived, but we didn't know that this was the everyday norm for him now.

When he came for dinner, it was generally filled with laughter at his latest adventure. Mike loved nice cars and expensive watches, so it wasn't unusual that each time he came to visit, there was a new watch or a new car with a fascinating story behind it. Mike was something of a hustler. He loved getting a 'good deal' on whatever had caught his fancy. He was jovial, happy to be with us, and extremely entertaining.

There was never a dull moment with Mike. On occasion, he would share how unhappy he was, and we would talk about it, but nothing ever changed. He would generally gloss over the unhappiness by joking about it—a common tactic to keep the darkness at bay.

Mike had always been a loving, helpful guy. He helped us out a lot over the years and did thoughtful things. He had always been a stand-up guy. As the drinking increased, a darker character came out.

There was a lot of cognitive dissonance for us as this character became increasingly cynical, transactional, and spiteful, in a passive-aggressive way. The way he began to talk about Naomi, the people that worked for him and some of his long-time friends was concerning. The happy-go-lucky Mike was disappearing, and what was emerging was a deeply unhappy person.

We tried talking with him about it; we wanted to understand where this was coming from in an attempt to help. Mike would share, we would listen and offer what we thought were helpful suggestions, and he would listen and leave our house ready to try a different way to deal with the situation, but nothing ever changed.

The alcohol was the easier route. Staying in the situation and drinking his way through it was the devil he knew. Change was too frightening for him to consider.

In fairness, we only saw Mike about once every month and half in those days, and so there wasn't a constant support system for him to lean on to make change manageable.

A few years after the move to the garage, he came over and was on fire to tell us about a rekindled romance he was having with a girlfriend he had when he was young. He had been on a trip to the UK, and they ran into each other. Apparently, the sparks were still there, and they began a torrid affair. He was so sure he was in love with her and that she was what had been missing his entire life. He traveled to the UK quite often then.

He was completely enraptured by the idea that he found his one true love and that this would change everything.

The dark Mike character was replaced with this lively, glowing bundle of energy that made him seem like a teenager. There was a spring in his step and light in his eyes that we had not seen in a long time. We thought that perhaps this might be a catalyst for him to finally make a change in his life.

All moral judgments aside, we were always rooting for our friend to find some peace and enjoyment in life.

He was still living in the garage and hiding all of this from his family, but he felt that he needed to be sure before he made any drastic changes. He was highly uncomfortable with the idea of leaving his sons, but the intoxication of 'being in love' was enough to keep him going back.

As compulsive, emotionally charged affairs often do, it ended badly. She didn't like that he drank so much, and that was the beginning of the end. As much as he was convinced of his love for her, the drinking served a more important purpose for him; we'll see what that was a bit later in the story.

He made one more trip to the UK to try to smooth it over; it didn't work. But when dealing with addictive behaviors, never fear—another fix is right around the corner. On his way back from that trip, he was flying business class and began flirting with the flight attendant. You guessed it, the next torrid affair was underway!

We would ask why he didn't just leave his family if these flings were what he wanted to pursue. Repeatedly, he would default to not wanting to hurt his boys. He would also assert that he was still taking care of the family and that was really his obligation, and so he deserved some happiness in his life for all the years he sacrificed by staying.

The flight attendant drank as much or more than he did, and soon, cocaine entered the picture. Since she was an international flight attendant, he didn't have to travel across the ocean as often to keep this one going because she was often here. The perfect recipe for disaster.

As you may have guessed, this one ended worse, as alcohol- and cocaine-fueled affairs generally do.

Mike would come over and tell us all the sordid details. The darker Mike was emerging again in the aftermath of these affairs. He was used to the coldness of his marriage, but rejection from these other women was a new affront to his character.

Unfortunately, Naomi found out about the flight attendant affair. When she asked Mike about it, to his credit, he told her the truth. As you can imagine, things at home were pretty uncomfortable for a while, but then the strangest thing happened.

When Naomi was faced with the knowledge that Mike was seeking others, and others found him desirable, she started paying attention to him. They began spending time together, both as a family and just the two of them watching a movie together on the couch. That soon led to sharing the same bed, which hadn't happened in years.

It's so interesting to watch the survival mechanisms engage.

Mike was Naomi's financial support. She didn't work full-time; she only had a part-time job doing something artistic. She did start a TikTok channel and was trying to be an influencer, so all the money she made at her part-time job went to Amazon to buy things to make videos about. She never got much of a following.

Naomi is pretty in a cold way. She takes care of her physical appearance and works out every day, but I've never heard anything of substance about her as a person. Mike would say she was a good mom, but that's about it. I have no knowledge of Naomi's underlying character or motivations; I can only write from my observation of behaviors.

It was fascinating to see the change in the relationship. Naomi's survival instinct kicked in, and she became attentive to Mike. Mike loved it. At his core, he was aching to be loved. He needed the attention, and she needed the support. It was a win-win situation as far as Mike was concerned.

Life went on this way for about a year and a half. Mike quit drinking. They took family vacations, Alex started working in the business with Mike, and to the outside eye, it looked like a happy family. We noticed that during this "family man" phase, the watches and cars were turning over at rapid speed. Then came the obsession with the crypto markets and stock options trading. It seemed to us that, not having the risk involved with sneaking around, the risk behavior presented itself in other ways.

Soon enough, neither Mike nor Naomi could keep up the appearance of a renewed relationship. The immediate danger of losing Mike was gone for Naomi, and Mike's addictive behaviors became his focal point once again. Drinking began to creep back into Mike's life. They stopped sharing a bed and he was once again living in the garage.

Mike became involved with an online group that gave stock, options, and crypto trading advice. His typical day would start at 5 a.m. so he could get online when the markets opened. He would spend the entire morning in his office watching the market and executing the trades of the day from the online group.

He didn't pay any attention to his business while the market was open. He allowed Alex to handle it and instructed the staff that he was not to be disturbed during those hours. He was doing well by all accounts in the markets and would come over and show us his portfolio.

One night, he was close to a million dollars. He said he couldn't wait until he hit the million so he could show his dad. The trading became Mike's obsession. The risk of it excited him. The reward when a trade went well was intoxicating; when a trade went badly, it energized him to double down on the next one. This became the only topic of conversation when we would see him.

We also began to notice that when he would arrive at our house, he was already drunk. When we asked about it, he freely admitted that yes, he had a few before coming, but that it was only his normal afternoon vodka. He was back to drinking most of the day. In his office, behind closed doors, playing the markets. It didn't help that his business was located next to a liquor store.

His appearance also began to change. He was bloated and he gained about 40 pounds. Mike had been one of those people who would go on an exercise routine for six months, feel great about it, but then something would happen—an injury or an emotional drama—and exercise would go out the window.

It was clear that during this period of his life, there was no exercise, most likely little food, and a lot of alcohol.

Mike was really flying high with the options trading, and his crypto portfolio was growing. With excess money coming in, Mike's spending kept up with it. He had this cockiness about him as if the amount of money he had made him more important.

He leased a couple of new cars: a Tesla for Naomi because he needed to keep up the appearance of taking care of her, and a BMW X5 for himself because that was the image he wanted to project.

It was around this same time that he went to visit his cousin who lived in Colombia. It is still a little unclear to us what the cousin did, but through innuendo and vague comments, we had the impression that whatever it was, it may not have been on the up-and-up.

He came to visit after his first trip to Colombia, and he was over the moon. Everything was awesome there! He just couldn't say enough about how amazing it was, and then it finally came out.

The time spent with his cousin was filled with cocaine, alcohol, and Viagra and many trips to the upper-class brothels. Not in the actual town his cousin lived in of course; these activities were carried out in the city while they were there 'on business' so the cousin's wife wouldn't be the wiser.

Mike was enamored with this lifestyle. He thought it was 'cool' and somehow showed that his cousin was 'successful.' He had it all.

Money, women, drugs, and life was a big party.

The Colombia trips became more frequent; he loved the party life. On one of these trips, he met a woman. She was 20 years younger than Mike, and once again, Mike thought he was in love.

How they met is unclear, either at a brothel or a club. There were actually two women in the beginning, he showed us pictures of both, but this one stole his heart.

The Colombian woman, Marisol, didn't speak any English. She was a 'former' prostitute, but now she made her living selling lingerie to other prostitutes. She had a large family and felt it was her responsibility to care for her nieces and nephews, and that costs money.

Mike would go to Colombia about once every month and a half. He would make up a story to tell Naomi about working out of town and often 'accidentally' leave his phone so she couldn't track him.

All Mike could talk about was Marisol. The stocks and crypto trading were still happening when he was home, but his mind was full of Marisol. He would say things like, "I mean, look at that body, and she likes me!" as if having a voluptuous body was a character trait. He was completely taken in by this little vixen.

Mike was completely blind to what was really happening. He would gush over how she made him feel and that she really cared about him. He was also convinced that this young woman needed to be taken care of, and he was the man for the job.

He began listening to Colombian music, he wore her perfume so that he smelled like her, and his every thought throughout the day was about Marisol and planning the next trip to see her. This one took over his life in a way we hadn't seen before.

He gave her a credit card, sent her money, and went down there as often as he could. They would go on cocaine-, booze- and Viagra-fueled sex fests that lasted days. Who wouldn't want that, right?

No matter how often we broached the subject that perhaps the relationship was more transactional than he realized, he wouldn't hear it. He would get defensive and tell us that clearly we didn't understand what it felt like to be loved after so long without.

He was convinced that they had a really deep connection and compared that connection to what he perceived with Lucas and me.

In the meantime, cocaine use became an everyday thing for Mike when he was home. He was strung out on alcohol and cocaine daily. The business was now faltering, the cracks were showing, and our friend was spiraling down at an alarming rate.

Mike came home from a trip to Colombia on Mother's Day. Dutifully, he bought Naomi flowers on the way home from the airport. That's what was strange about the whole thing: Mike was emotionally distant with his family, but he always made sure they were cared for.

He took care of everything on a financial level and made sure birthdays and holidays were celebrated for them. It wasn't even a question for him. It wasn't just about keeping up appearances to hide his affair, it was his genuine responsibility to look after the family, and so he did.

Mike walked in the door with the flowers, handed them to Naomi and she promptly threw them at him. Naomi had the password to Mike's phone and since he conveniently left it home, she went snooping. She saw every text and every picture. She knew it all. The shit had hit the fan. Happy Mother's Day indeed.

While there was much yelling and blaming, neither Mike nor Naomi took any action. Naomi didn't leave or kick him out, and Mike didn't consider leaving either. It wasn't an option in their minds to simply end this disaster of a relationship.

Mike didn't stop going to Colombia. Naomi took no action, and it was back to 'normal,' except this time, Mike found an app that would make it look like he was where he said he was should Naomi think about tracking his phone. Problem solved.

On his next trip to Colombia, he told Naomi he was working out of town. He used the app and was satisfied that Naomi was none the wiser. It apparently worked because there were no questions when he got back home except to ask how the 'job' had gone. This was now a high-tech affair.

The next time Mike went to Colombia, he roped in a co-conspirator. He had a contractor working for him named Scott. He told Scott that he had informed Naomi that Scott was going with him for an out-of-town job. He asked Scott not to contact anyone at the business during the time Mike would be away; it was important that the lie held up. Scott agreed to this.

Unfortunately, Naomi ran into Scott at the grocery store of all places. They had most likely never run into each other in all the years they lived here, but here he was, when he was supposed to be out of town on a job with Mike. Scott spilled the beans. The lie was uncovered, and the jig was up.

Both Naomi and Scott were texting Mike furiously on his last day in Colombia before he was to return home. Mike knew the walls were caving in. His answer to that was to get seriously blasted, so he passed out on the flight home.

Immediately upon his return, the family and a couple who were considered friends of the family held an intervention. They gave Mike an ultimatum: He had to go to an in-patient rehab center, or he had to move out. The couple, Clark and Martha, and the oldest son, Alex, would take care of the business for him while he was gone. The important thing was for him to get help.

The messaging wasn't about the affair with Marisol; it was all about the drinking and drugs. That's what he needed to deal with. Out of their utmost concern for Mike, they demanded the in-patient center; it was all set up, and they were really rooting for him to get better—or so it seemed at the time.

He sent us a text explaining that he would be in rehab for thirty days and wouldn't have access to his phone but would reach out when he got back.

The weekend before Thanksgiving, we got a call from Mike. He was due to get out of rehab the day before Thanksgiving, and his family had notified him that he was not allowed to come back home. So much for taking care of things for him so he could get help. It was a ruse to passively aggressively kick him out of the home and steal the business. More on that later.

He asked if he could stay with us for a few days until he figured things out. Those few days turned into six months.

Lucas picked Mike up from rehab at the appointed time. This Mike was tearful, fearful, and shaken. When they arrived home, Mike would cry every time he tried to speak.

He couldn't thank us enough because the reality was he had nowhere else to go. He told us that when he got the news that his family didn't want him to come home, he went through the list of people he could call; we were the only ones he knew for sure would help him. That alone is a sobering realization.

Living in a place for over 25 years, and when push comes to shove, all the people you thought were your friends were just surface acquaintances.

That first night was just about giving Mike space and time to adjust to the new reality. The facility he had been in was one where most folks were there under court order. They slept eight to a room and shared a bathroom at the end of the hall. The daily routine was very structured, similar to prison. Mike hadn't had his own space in a month. He said he felt 'exposed' and scared.

We had never seen Mike like this. It was a little shocking. That night, he needed a lot of tender loving care. We hugged him a lot and let him cry without needing to explain or stop. There were 53 years of repressed emotions coming out of him, and the best thing we could do was let them flow. He just kept saying over and over again that he was scared. It was heartbreaking.

Thanksgiving Day we had some friends over for the traditional fried turkey and carb-loaded side dishes that the day is known for. Upon their arrival, the tearful Mike from the night before morphed into Mike the Entertainer. He had an audience. The change was striking to behold. The character adapting to the environment in real time.

In his trademark charming way, he began to tell the tale of rehab. The way he spoke, you would have thought he had been there for a year instead of a month.

First off was a detailed explanation of the mess hall menu and how he hadn't had 'real food' in *'so long,'* and it was as if he could taste for the first time! He regaled us with stories about the 'mates' he made in rehab. "Proper Cholo's," as he put it, who had been in prison!

How he had a severe case of gout and was in a wheelchair for the first two weeks, but his 'mates' took right good care of him. He learned that in prison, before you get up from the table, you knock on it so that no one thinks it's a sudden move that could be threatening.

Of course, Mike began to knock on the table before he got up from eating; that lasted about a week.

He gushed on and on about the *amazing* guys in there and about how he discovered journaling and that he was writing some *really great* stuff and now he wanted to make it into a book because the insights were so profound. He just couldn't stop writing! He told us, "I woke up early just so I could write; I found so much out about myself, it really helped me kick this alcohol thing."

Mike was convinced that he was cured of his addiction to alcohol and now understood everything so he could get his life together, and get back to his business, and heal the relationship with his kids.

The following few days, he raved about how free he felt now. He realized that he was unhappy and that's what was driving him to drink, so he decided he was going to broaden his horizons and find what really made him happy.

He considered going into acting because he always thought he would be good at it; he spoke at length about how to publish his book and even began typing it up. He had this mania about him. The world was his oyster now, and he could do anything!

He was very intent on the idea that his book would really help people. He knew he had the most profound insights that would help even the most desperate. He had learned so much in those thirty days, and he needed to share it.

He was also obsessed with taking care of his 'mates' he met on the 'inside.' He took loads of clothes and shoes to them, loaned them money when they got out, and got messages to their friends for them while they were still in.

This was a remarkable example of the chameleon Ego character; his identity took on the shape of a rehab inmate in record time and continued for a time after he was out.

While in rehab, he had one of his 'mates' draw up his next tattoo for him, and he was super excited to get it. There was tremendous importance placed on getting this tattoo. He needed a change of costume for the new identity of Mike, the Rehab Survivor. His attention to this was obsessive. It was another strange thing to us. He'd lost everything but was obsessed with getting another tattoo.

He never got it done. It was just an avoidance tactic to obsess over while the Ego identity was reshaping itself.

Outwardly, it looked like he was flying high, excited about getting himself together, getting back to work, and getting his life in order. He even bought himself a new, expensive watch as a reward for completing the rehab program. He let us know that it was important to him to treat himself when he accomplished things.

The reality of this behavior was the character appropriating a sober, successfully healed former addict, not understanding that the watch purchase was simply another behavior driven by addiction.

He reminded us of folks who get back from their first spiritual or self-help retreats. Full of energy, a no-holds-barred belief that they've broken the code and that life is going to be amazing now. Everything has changed, and it's all been figured out, and the need to share is a driving force.

As generally happens, that high takes about three weeks to dissolve, and it was no different for Mike, except it was about a week and a half. Mike was in the first stage of 'fake awake.' It generally has a little bit of mania attached to it, as the excitement of new information and identity shaping around it is too much to keep inside.

We were baffled by the Mike character that was now inhabiting our home. Here was a man who has lost nearly everything, and that didn't seem to be registering. He was jovial, funny, and excited to 'get back out there.' It wasn't what we had expected, and we saw that the reality had not set in for him and had serious concerns about that.

We had no idea what the following months would bring.

After a week and a half, Mike felt ready to pick up his things from his former home. He had a brave face outwardly but also asked Lucas to go with him. When he got there, all of his belongings were in trash bags on the side of the street, like so much garbage. This was the first visible crack in the fake awake façade.

The family had left the key under the mat for him in case they forgot to put any of his things out. They were away for this pre-arranged pickup. Lucas described watching Mike melt down when they walked into the house. His two small dogs excitedly greeted him, and Mike fell to pieces.

All he could do was walk around the house as if in a daze.

The reality of the situation was beginning to become clear. Lucas gently prodded Mike to get his things loaded up and drove him back to our house. This was a different Mike. This Mike was shattered for the trip home. It was a Fracture Point.

Interestingly, when they got home and started loading bags and bags of things into his room, Mike became excited again. Excited to 'move in' to his room and get it set up. The defenses successfully morphed the shattered Mike into the exited Mike during the short ride home.

There was a dampening of his sparkle that he was trying desperately to hide, but the character took over in stunning fashion, resulting in a flurry of activity to get the room sorted.

This was the first time we had a glimpse into the many addictions that Mike was dealing with. He brought in about 150 pairs of shoes.

Some were never worn, yet new packages were showing up daily. More shoes, shirts, jeans—all brand-name things—though his room was stuffed to the brim.

Mike spent about three days obsessing over getting his room set up. It was like watching a thirteen-year-old who had never had a room of his own. The sheer excitement in him was strange to behold. The shoes that *had* been worn all got a thorough cleaning so that they gleamed when he put them back on the shelf.

He even offered to clean *our* shoes; he was so attached to the activity. I will add that our shoes never looked better after Mike got to them. He would leave them lined up on the stairs, *displayed* for us to see. He would then explain in great detail the step-by-step process to properly clean athletic shoes.

The manic cleaning and organizing were clearly an avoidance tactic. Finding his things in garbage bags hit him hard, and he was not ready to deal with what all that meant. So, he cleaned, organized, and bought more things.

During these first couple of weeks, he was obsessively cleaning our house as well—vacuuming, cleaning the bathroom, washing all the rugs, and doing the dishes. He was trying to stay busy all day.

The interesting thing is that each evening, he would then tell us all the things he did. "I vacuumed the stairs today, did you notice?" "I wiped down the refrigerator, did you notice?" When we would say "Thank you," he would respond, "You don't need to thank me, I just want you to know I did it."

Our household has a peaceful, easy flow to it. Lucas and I flow effortlessly together. Things get done. The house gets cleaned, food gets made, work happens and all without perceived effort. Having

Mike, the Manic Maid, in the house was a disruption to that flow that we hadn't seen coming.

During this period, Clark and Martha sent an email to Mike to communicate that they weren't comfortable YET with him returning to the business or home. He needed to enroll in an outpatient rehab to continue his work, and then they would consider whether he could come back to the business he built from the ground up or have any contact with his family.

You read that right: *Clark and Martha* would decide these things for both for Mike and his family.

They made it clear to Mike that the family wanted no contact with him until he finished the outpatient program. The crazy thing is, we have no idea if this is how the family felt or wanted to handle it.

Clark and Martha had forbidden the family to contact Mike. I can't speak to how a grown woman like Naomi, or her grown sons, would allow other people to dictate how they handled their own business. But all communication was from Clark and Martha.

This particular message was worded in a way that led Mike to believe that if he just did this outpatient therapy and finished it, he would then be reintegrated into the business and have some kind of relationship with his children. They assured him the business was running well and there was nothing for him to worry about on that front. He just needed to continue his 'healing journey.'

Mike took them at their word, and for his part, as much as he was able, he was willing to do whatever they asked. He enrolled in the outpatient program and began going six days a week just before Christmas.

The original 'high' of getting out of rehab was wearing off, and he was once again committed to doing the work laid out for him.

He began to write again; journaling really seemed to help him get the thoughts out of his head, and he always felt better after a writing session. He would take his notebook and write in the daily classes as well. We would have long talks each evening about what he was discovering, and he would tell us how well he was doing and how much it was helping him realize things about himself.

When Mike wanted our input, we gladly gave it. We weren't easy on him; we didn't coddle him. We told him hard things, but in a loving way. He would share his insights with us in the evening, and we would discuss and give him our perspective. This was helpful to him, he said, because he felt safe with us.

He told us intensely personal things and how those things affected him. We would discuss from our perspective, and his eyes were opening to an entirely different viewpoint of the events surrounding his story.

During this time, we learned that Mike hadn't just given up alcohol and cocaine; he had also been on four different prescription medications for anxiety and depression, including benzos. This was news to us. We had no idea he had been on medication for the last six years. He had never shared this with us before.

As Mike's walls came down and he began to share these things with us, and we settled into the routine of him living in our home, we began to see the signs that Mike really had no idea how to care for himself. He was very disconnected from his body, it seemed.

Here was a man that had just kicked several substances cold turkey, and his body was in chaos.

He couldn't make the simplest connections between his diet and physical reactions in his body. It's not something he ever paid attention to. He had stomach issues, acid reflux, insomnia, rashes on his skin, and serious gout flare-ups in the first month he was with us.

He lived on sugar-laden cereal in the morning, two or three mochaccinos from Starbucks a day, maybe a small sandwich for lunch, candy bars, donuts and muffins throughout the day, and then he would eat a small dinner because he didn't have an appetite and his stomach was upset. He popped antacids several times a day.

We began to work with him on his diet, as he seemed to have no idea that what he ate could cause these flare-ups in his body. He hadn't even considered that kicking all the substances at once would be shocking to the body's homeostasis. There was no connection to his body at all. It just had symptoms, and he treated those symptoms as best he could.

A couple of weeks before Christmas, we awoke to Mike knocking on our bedroom door at 5 a.m. because he had a major gout flare up and the pain was unbearable. He asked Lucas to drive him to the hospital to get medication and "something for the pain." This was such a dramatic event. If it had been an actor in a movie, we would have said it was very "overacted." But this was Mike. Everything was extremely dramatic, all the time.

Lucas drove him to the hospital, and he got what he thought he needed. Most importantly, he got pain medication. That's what all the drama was about, really. The body–mind conspiracy. One of the tricks of the Ego character under attack is to create symptoms and/or pain.

Having been clean for over a month, the body found a way to get a little fix. I'm not saying gout isn't super painful and that pain medication treatment isn't called for. I'm simply making an interesting observation about the severity of the drama surrounding the appearance of gout.

It took a good five days for it to calm down to the point that he could walk without pain. In the meantime, he wore a boot, like the ones folks use after a broken ankle. The entire week before Christmas, the only subject of conversation was Mike's gout and Mike's pain; or rather, Mike's story about it. There was plenty of "I can't believe this is happening to me, I've already been through so much!"

It was as if he thought there was some universal force "out there," punishing him beyond what he could handle.

During the gout recovery phase, he was advised not to eat red meat. We made chicken in about a hundred different ways for the next three weeks! I think our next book will be a cookbook titled something like, "Roost to Roast: The Sacred Art of Chicken."

We had to get very creative. Lucas and I like good food, and we both enjoy cooking, but using the same protein for three weeks in a row was challenge, even for us. However, we were very committed to helping Mike in any way that we could, and we supported his dietary needs, teaching him about fueling his body rather than pumping it full of sugar all day, every day.

Mike was very childlike in his excitement to learn these things. At 53 years old, he knew so little about simply living and taking care of his body. It was like having a 10-year-old in the house who was curious to learn but needed instruction on just about everything.

Once the diet was addressed, Mike didn't have another gout episode for the rest of the time he was with us. His digestion improved; he didn't have acid reflux, and his skin rash cleared up in a few weeks. Giving his body fuel provided Mike with a more solid foundation to continue the work he needed to do. His brain was sharper, he slept better, and things were looking up.

Mike needed a tremendous amount of care. That was something we hadn't anticipated, but we were happy that we had the space and the time to help him. This wasn't the Mike we thought we knew all those years. The character he had played for us was not the same character we had now, nor was it the same character he showed the rest of the world.

Christmas came, and Mike had been telling us the entire week leading up to it that it was going to be a hard day for him. We cautioned him against setting it up that way, telling him he had no idea if it was going to be a hard day because it wasn't here. In all honesty, the only reason we even know the days is that they are represented as squares on a calendar.

It's really just a day, but we feed it with emotional attachment.

In between fretting about how hard Christmas Day was going to be, Mike had bouts of complete, unadulterated excitement about the gift he had gotten for us. When Mike was excited, he couldn't hold it in. He would talk about it, how excited he was for us to open it, and begin giving hints as if it was just too awesome to keep inside. We would repeatedly shut him down. "Shut up about it, Mike! You're going to ruin the surprise!" It became an ongoing joke. He would start to say something, and we would immediately say, "Shhhhhhh!" There was as much laughter as there was fretting.

We had our Christmas and included Mike as part of the family. We take turns opening gifts in our house. He had his pile of gifts to open and teared up with each one. They weren't expensive, but they were meaningful, and he was overwhelmed.

He told us that as an adult, he had never received a Christmas gift. In his house, it was all about the kids and Naomi. He was really taken aback by the small gifts he received.

We saved Mike's gift to us for last. It was a large box that he had managed to wrap and carry up the stairs to sit next to the tree. It contained two outdoor patio chairs. Lucas and I spend a lot of time sitting outside when the weather allows, and it always bothered Mike that we didn't have chairs with cushions.

It was an extremely thoughtful and appreciated gift that we still use every day. The best part was Mike's reaction to our reaction. It brought him so much joy to have gotten us something that we will use and appreciate.

It was a glimpse of our old friend. He and Lucas put the chairs together, and they were the perfect size, the perfect fit and the perfect color. We love them.

All in all, the day was quite wonderful. We had our traditional meat and cheese fondue for dinner, and Mike really enjoyed the day. It wasn't until the evening hours that the day became hard.

He began ruminating in his thoughts that it was CHRISTMAS and he hadn't heard from his sons. He had an expectation that he would at least get some kind of message from them because reaching out to your family is kind of an obligation on holidays, right? He sank deep into this narrative and was visibly down through New Year's.

A few days after Christmas, Mike's mom came to visit. She was visiting from the UK and staying with his family. He picked her up and brought her over for a little dinner party we had with some other friends from out of town in attendance.

This was the first time we had met his mom. She had a lovely calmness about her. It was interesting to observe Mike with her. At first, he was super excited to show her his room, again it felt like a child's behavior. "Come see my room, Mom!"

Mike, the Entertainer, did not make an appearance this time. As the evening progressed, he became more withdrawn and sulkier, even snapping at his mom. Everyone else was having a lovely time, taking our time, chatting over after-dinner espresso. Mike abruptly left the table to go sulk in the next room.

I went to check on him, and he was just sitting there staring into space. When I asked him what was wrong, he said he thought his gout might be flaring up again and that he was tired, and he still had to take his mom back, so she should hurry it up. I told him that we would be glad to get her home if he needed to rest. He sniffed at that.

It was confusing, but I think it somehow had something to do with his mom having a wonderful time with other people, as if he was feeling invisible because everyone was chatting away and it wasn't about him.

After about ten minutes, he came to the table and told his mother to get her things; they were leaving. It was rude, petulant and completely unnecessary. His mom dutifully cut the evening short and prepared to leave. When they got to the door, Mike was already running out the door, down our very steep porch steps, leaving his 80-year-old mother to navigate them on her own.

Lucas took her arm and carefully helped her down the stairs, and this didn't sit well with Mike. "I can help my own mother!" he said in a very snarky tone. Lucas just calmly replied, "Yes, you can, but you didn't." Mike left in a huff, and when he returned, he went straight to his room without another word.

Lucas and I were dumbfounded. It was like having a troubled preteen living with us, complete with confusing drama and out-of-the-blue mood swings.

New Year's Eve came, another day that Mike insisted was going to be hard for him because it always had been. When we questioned him on this, he said it was because of all the "new year, new me" bullshit everyone spouts. He said it always reminded him that he had accomplished nothing in the year.

Again, we suggested that we didn't have to put so much pressure on a square on a calendar and that it was possible to simply enjoy the day when it came.

Lucas and I have a simple tradition for New Year's Eve. We put a pot roast in the crock pot and proceed to watch all three extended versions of the Lord of the Rings trilogy and time it so it ends just before midnight. Mike thought he could do that with us. He had never seen the movies, and it sounded fun and not too stressful.

About halfway through the first movie, Mike began getting agitated. He was up and down, pacing, couldn't sit still on the couch, obsessively looking at his phone, pacing some more, going up to his room, coming back down, filling the house with anxious, nervous energy.

When we asked him if he was okay, he just said, "This day is always bad for me, and I know I'm bad company, so I'm not going to watch the rest of it and ruin your day, I'll just go to my room."

We found out later that everything was going fine until he got a text from Marisol. She was begging him to buy her a car and come to see her. That really sent him into a spiral. He was still communicating with her every day, still sending money, though he was running out of it.

It seemed her neediness both annoyed and put pressure on him.

He wanted to be able to give her everything she asked for; he somehow felt obligated, but he wasn't in a position to do those things. This was really a distraction from the work he needed to do for himself. It clouded his mind.

After the holidays, things calmed down, and Mike was going to his daily outpatient recovery classes, and then he would come home and journal for the afternoon. He wasn't obsessively cleaning any longer, but he did ask that we leave the kitchen for him to clean in the afternoons after his journaling.

As far as house guests go, Mike was extremely conscientious about cleaning up after himself and, to some extent, our son, with whom he shared a bathroom. He was always willing to help with the household chores. It was important to him to contribute to the household however he could.

Mike seemed to be enjoying the outpatient classes each day, and his journaling was helping him see some things that we would again sit and discuss in the evenings. There was a rhythm to it, and he seemed to be excited, committed to the work, and making progress. He was beginning to see how drinking had affected his life and his decisions.

He had many insights during this first month of therapy, writing, and discussions with us. He was somewhat enjoying the process because it was the first time in his life that he questioned anything about himself, his beliefs, his thoughts, or his addictions.

All our input was from our experience of seeing Ego structure and Ego character and how it functions. These were things that we had alluded to throughout our years of friendship, but we never went too deep because there was no connection to it for Mike. Now, however, he couldn't get enough. He was gaining insights at a rapid rate, which can happen when you have nothing else to do.

To his credit, he put all he had into this outpatient therapy work for about a month.

During all this time, Mike was still in daily contact with Marisol, still convinced he was in love with her. His commitment to the program was driven by wanting to get better first for her and then for his sons. At this stage, it was more about her than them. I think he shifted his focus to her because it was unclear when or if his sons would agree to have contact with him.

There was this big, unknown void regarding his family as there had been no contact up to this point. As an avoidance tactic, his sole focus shifted to doing this for Marisol.

Marisol was still asking for money, and Mike was gladly sending it. Though without income, he had a swiftly dwindling supply. The cocaine binges and market collapse had all but wiped out his stock and crypto portfolio by the time he went to rehab.

As much as Mike freely admitted he also had a "love addiction" according to a book he looked at in his therapist's office, he still could not see what the situation with Marisol really was.

The signs of Ego reinventing itself started appearing around the second month of the program. Mike began coming home from therapy telling us how he was so much more advanced than anyone else there. He chalked that up to having nightly talks with us. He would say things like, "My understanding is so much deeper. I know more than the therapists at this place; I give better advice to others in the group sessions than they do!"

This development was concerning for us because we knew that all that was really happening was that the Ego character was learning a new language. It was appropriating and morphing into the "awakened" one, and all those other people were just floundering in their lack of understanding.

We constantly confronted this, but Ego character does what it does.

Mike now had words and language that he was parroting to his fellow recovering addicts and became the wise one in the group. He had no understanding at all at this point, only new, fun words that made him the one everyone wanted to seek out. The British accent didn't hurt here; to American ears, it sounds so much smarter than the way Bubba from Alabama would articulate the information.

This was a deepening of the fake awake stage, very similar to spiritual seekers claiming awakening. Most are just parroting whatever the guru of the month is selling and have no understanding at all. It's just the Ego appropriating the spiritual character with the language that sounds legitimate in those circles. A lot of books and courses are created at this deeper fake awake stage, and millions lap it up.

As the second month progressed, Mike's resistance became more pronounced. He was very sure of himself; he didn't want to talk about things anymore because he had this addiction thing beat. He felt strong and believed that alcohol or drugs would no longer hold any temptation for him. He also stopped asking for our advice on things and stopped writing. He told us in no uncertain terms that it was time for him to take back control of his own life and make his own decisions.

We could see clearly that he was setting the stage to return to Colombia.

He graduated from his outpatient program. He was very proud of that, received the certificate, emailed his family to tell them he'd done it and immediately booked a flight to Colombia.

We both knew this was coming. He was like an open book to us now. He couldn't hide much from us for long; we generally knew when he was lying or scheming something, and this was no different. Lucas and I discussed it and concluded that there was really nothing we could do.

Mike is an adult, and our home was not a prison. We were both very concerned because we could see what was happening and knew he would spiral again.

A couple of days after Lucas and I discussed the possibility of the Colombia trip, Mike asked if he could take us out to Sushi as a "thank you" for all we had done for him. We both knew this was a setup—a clumsy attempt to get on neutral ground.

Mike was anxious at dinner; he didn't have an appetite, and he became very quiet once we were seated. After about fifteen minutes, he finally blurted out that he really appreciated everything we had done for him but that he was better now and had made the decision to go to Colombia.

We both turned to him and said, "We know." He was dumbfounded. He worked himself up to all of this, and all the while, we both knew what was coming. We told him it was a really bad idea in no uncertain terms. We were concerned that he would be alone in an environment full of temptation. We could see what he could not, which is often the case.

Rather than fight him on it, we encouraged him to reconsider, but if he decided to go, to take his journals and keep up his writing. We also made sure he knew that we were just a phone call away if he got into a situation where he was tempted to drink.

Mike went to Colombia.

He texted us when he got there to let us know he made it, and we didn't hear from him for the next two weeks until it was time to give us the information to pick him up at the airport.

We both suspected that sobriety had been abandoned.

When Mike returned, Mike, the Entertainer, was back in full force. He told us about his trip and what an absolutely wonderful time he had; so good, in fact that he had already scheduled another trip to go back in three weeks' time. He was over the moon about Marisol and told us how much he loved her and that she loved him and took really good care of him while he was there.

He shared with us that yes, he did drink a little because he needed to prove to himself that he didn't need it anymore.

When we asked if he only drank once, he said, "No, I knew I could handle it, so I had a little each evening." Warning bells were going off in our heads. We pressed the issue, "So, if you didn't need it after the first time, why did you continue to drink? If the first time was to prove it to yourself, then what was every other drink about?" All he would answer was, "I like to have a little bit of wine with dinner, and I was okay with it."

By this time, Lucas and I could tell when Character Mike was lying. We both knew that much more occurred on that trip than what Mike was sharing.

Two days after Mike came home, he asked to take us to dinner again, and we agreed. As soon as we sat down, Mike ordered a bottle of wine. Neither of us said anything about the wine; we wanted to see how this played out.

Mike was extremely talkative, gushing over how wonderful the trip was, especially being with Marisol again. He talked non-stop about how he was blown away by how it felt to be *LOVED* by someone else. "I think she really loves me," he said. "When we have dinner, she always gives me a bite off of her fork, little things like that let me know that she really cares about me."

About this time, Mike ordered a second bottle of wine; the food had not yet come to the table.

Mike was getting tipsy, and that led him to open up and tell us intimate details of an experience he had with Marisol while they were there. "I had some Cialis with me, and since it had been a while, I took two. After dinner and a few drinks, we were having sex, and I had this strange experience of watching us from the upper corner of the room! Like, I wasn't even in my body!" "It was *really cool* but then I got freaked out and my heart started pounding, my head felt like it was going to explode, and I had to stop. I really wasn't feeling well; Marisol gave me some water and then she was going to call an ambulance, but I told her I would be fine. It was quite a few hours before I felt better, and I was still not 100% the next day, but I was okay."

Dinner was now finished, and Mike ordered another bottle of wine to have with dessert. Clearly, Mike's claim that he could handle a little wine with dinner was proving to be false.

We drove him home and knew that the next day we were going to have to address the issue of Mike drinking.

The next day, Lucas broached the subject of drinking with Mike. Mike was defensive and didn't think that three bottles of wine for a "celebration" of his return home was excessive, but he understood our concern. He added, "I don't feel the need to drink at home; that was just a one-time thing."

The "one-time thing" turned into him asking if we needed anything about every other day. We weren't keeping alcohol in the house except when another friend of ours came to visit on weekends. We would buy beer for him. Mike would say, "Is Jim coming to visit this weekend? Do you want me to go get some beer?" When we said, "No, thank you," he would then go on to explain, "I don't want it for me, I'm just trying to be helpful because I know you're so busy." We knew better.

For the week after he returned, Mike began talking about getting his own place to live. He didn't want to be a burden to us any longer, and he needed to start living his life again. He made a couple of trips to look at rooms for rent and even fantasized about living on a boat. He went so far as to look at a couple of boats for sale, and he would spend these evening conversations talking about how cool that would be. "I've always wanted to live on a boat, and now I can do it!"

His energy felt "off" to us. There was something going on with him that made both of us want to avoid him. It was like he was living in a fantasy world that we couldn't see. We were still supporting him because his funds were running low, and most of what he talked about was the next trip to Colombia, Marisol, and looking for his own place.

It was like he completely forgot that he had no money, no job, no contact with his family, and that there were very adult things that needed to be dealt with. There was still the car lease payment, insurance, cell phone bill, and some outstanding debts that needed to be taken care of. There were also decisions to be made about his business and his marriage. He didn't talk about those things, only his big dreams and his love for Marisol.

We also started noticing the extreme amount of outside validation that Mike required. He had a new pair of shoes from Colombia, and he asked me if I liked them, I said, "Not particularly, not really my thing. But it doesn't matter if I like them or not; it matters if you do." He got very quiet, and within an hour had gone upstairs and changed; I never saw him wear those shoes again.

There was also one morning that I told him I liked his shirt. He gushed, "Oh, you do? You really like it?" I assured him that I did.

He bought three more exactly the same and wore them nearly every day.

Without having the daily outpatient rehab classes to go to any longer, Mike had very little to do during the day, except go look at boats and rooms for rent. He spent most of his time in his room watching TV. He would come down about 5 p.m. and do the dishes, that was still important to him. He would spend an hour or two telling us all his big dreams while we were preparing dinner and then take his food up to his room and continue watching TV.

We suspected that during his outings to look at boats and apartments, he was having a drink or five. He began wearing excessive amounts of cologne, enough to make us gag—the kind that lingered for hours. It was repulsive and hard to be in the same room with him.

We had begun to tiptoe around our own house. The fantasy world, cologne-soaked, sleezy feeling Mike was something we both were actively avoiding. We wanted to be very quiet so as not to wake him. Once this Mike character entered a room, it was disruptive and so full of bullshit that neither of us really had the energy to deal with it.

Lucas and I had some long conversations about the situation. We were not here just to feed and shelter him for the rest of his life while he continued to live in his addiction. For us, this was difficult. We knew he had nowhere to go, we knew he had no money, and so what were we going to do? Kick him out? Where would he go? We began looking into sober living houses that might be able to help him and thought that they might be the best solution for him —and for us.

On a Tuesday morning, about a week before his next trip to Colombia was scheduled, I was getting ready to go to work when Mike came into the kitchen. He once again parroted, "I really think I'm going to get an apartment. I looked at some online last night." At that moment, something in me took over.

I said, "Yes, I think you should, and you should do it soon. A better idea would be a sober living place because you clearly need help, and you no longer see it." Mike looked at me like a deer in the headlights and said in a small voice, "You don't want me here anymore?" I went on a rant.

"Mike is very welcome here, but Mike's addictions are not. You are losing it, my friend. Was the first time in rehab not enough for you? Was losing your family, your home, and your business not enough for you? Because if it wasn't, I don't really want to be around to watch what it will take for you. How low do you have to sink before you really get serious about this?"

Mike replied tearfully, "I am trying, I know I need help, I want to get better for my boys, and I just don't know what to do." I had no patience for the little victim act because that's how I saw it, an act.

"YOUR BOYS? That's bullshit, and you know it. Did you give a shit about them when you went on your alcohol, cocaine, and Cialis-fueled Colombian f@ck fest? Because that's all you seem to talk about, not your boys. Are you going to Colombia again for your boys? I'm sure they appreciate your efforts!"

I continued: "You can't even see that Marisol is just another addiction for you. She's using you for money; that's what it amounts to, and you are using her to stroke your addiction. A match made in heaven. If you cared about her the way you say you do, you would cut off all contact with her and focus on getting to the bottom of why, at 53 years old, you are living in our house with no money, no business, no family, no home, and all you can think about is getting your next high—whether that's Marisol or another watch or a new pair of shoes or the next drink or some cocaine. THAT's what you need to focus on."

Mike was shocked. Now it felt like I was talking to Mike and not the little victim. He said, "What do I have to do to stay here? Please tell me what I need to do, and I'll do it." "You're right, I'm not ok. I spiraled into the same things when I was in Colombia. I drank more than I let on and I did do cocaine. I need help; tell me what I have to do."

I said, "The very first thing you need to do is cut off all contact with Marisol. Lose her number. You will not be going to Colombia next week. Then, you need to either go back to inpatient rehab for another 30 days or back to your outpatient rehab here for another round. Lucas is willing to do some work with you as well, in addition to your rehab, and you need to get a therapist for private sessions at least once a week. If you can commit to those things, you can stay."

I continued, "We care, Mike. We are willing to help you, but at the end of the day, the work is yours, and you have to do it."

Mike tearfully said he would call the rehab center immediately. I gave him a hug, and I went to work.

Lucas had heard all of this go down. Right after I left, Mike went into Lucas's office. Lucas described it like this: "I had never seen him that distraught. He was completely broken. He was crying like a child who just got told his parents were getting a divorce. It was visceral."

Mike asked Lucas if he would help him. Lucas said that he would, but this was the last chance. He told Mike, "Everything that Shadow said was right on point, Mike. If you really want to get serious and get yourself together, then the outpatient therapy, a private therapist, and, most importantly, no contact with Marisol are the requirements. If you're willing to meet those requirements, we are more than willing to try to help you." Mike agreed to the conditions.

Mike started another round of outpatient rehab the very next day. He had an appointment with a therapist for the following week, and we gave him until the weekend to write a letter to Marisol and tell her there would be no further contact. Then the work with Lucas would begin.

Mike opened up and told us the truth about the trip to Colombia. He said he drank every day, even though his body was in distress after the first sip. He had acid reflux and was eating Tums like candy; he felt terrible in the mornings and the only thing that seemed to help was to have a beer immediately upon waking up, followed by more Tums.

As the trip progressed, cocaine came back into the picture as well. Mike had so much self-hatred over this. He had really believed that he could control it, that he was "healed," and that he was too strong for the temptation.

The reality is that alcohol and cocaine were the foundation of the relationship with Marisol. Without those binding agents, it was unlikely that the "deep connection" he described would have developed at all. Mike doesn't speak Spanish and Marisol doesn't speak English, alcohol, cocaine and sex were the mediums of communication, and without those things, the relationship didn't exist.

He had a fairy tale in his head not realizing that the whole story depended on the poison apple.

Mike struggled with writing the letter to Marisol. He obsessed over what to say to her. He still had some feeling of responsibility toward her and felt like he was just another guy abandoning her.

Marisol had told Mike her victim story of always being abandoned; that's why she had to go into prostitution. But she was working hard now to support herself in other ways, though of course, she always needed more money than she could make honestly.

Mike was the perfect target for this kind of con. He had a fantasy that he was going to save her and take care of her when he couldn't save or take care of himself or the family he already had. Marisol milked this savior complex and knew what buttons to push with Mike.

He was hooked on the idea of her; this addiction was stronger than alcohol and drugs combined for him.

Sunday came, and Mike sent the letter to Marisol; he also deleted her pictures off his phone and laptop, which he proudly showed us. He said he felt relieved and that he could see now how much energy keeping up that relationship took. He was committed and ready to do the work to get his life together without her as a distraction.

Lucas began to work with Mike on Monday. The daily schedule looked something like this:

In the gym by 7 a.m. for a workout. Mike went to outpatient rehab at 10 a.m. and was home by 1 p.m. He took an hour to himself to process the work done that day or take a short nap.

Lucas provided a manilla envelope to Mike with the day's assignment. Mike spent about 4 hours on the assignments; Lucas was always available if he needed help.

At 6 p.m., Mike would come down and discuss what came up for him during the day.

There was also the requirement that once a week, usually Sundays, Mike was responsible for preparing dinner.

The assignments were mostly writing assignments to help Mike excavate his thoughts, feelings, beliefs, and assumptions that were running as a pattern in his life.

There was a guiding question on a topic, such as "Who did you look up to in your family when you were young," and then instructions on how to dissect the surface answers and go deeper into the "why".

The work Lucas lined out for Mike was the beginning of what would later become "Lenswork – The Sacred Work of Self-Destruction" Rupture Workbook. The process was based on work that both Lucas and I had done that brought us to the realizations of the Ego structure, Ego character, and how the simulation worked.

We weren't working with Mike about "Awakening"; we simply used the Lenswork method to address addictions and behaviors for Mike to gain insight into his own life. The process is the same no matter what the issue is.

We were brutally honest with Mike about this work. We told him from our experience that unearthing the Ego structure is like a prizefight for your life. When he would insist he was ready, we told him in no uncertain terms that he had no idea what he was going up against.

The Ego structure and the simulation will strike back; the body will rebel, and the mind will play tricks. We warned him that the work was difficult, unsettling to the character, and that some days would feel like the end of the world.

Mike was undeterred. He wasn't willing to go on without getting to the bottom of the issue so that he could rebuild his life.

The first week focused on Mike's relationship with alcohol. He realized that he was using it as a numbing agent. Mike had never learned how to process emotions of any kind; he began drinking very early in life. Some of that just seemed like his culture, but as the work continued, he realized that it was the numbing effect of problematic emotions that drove it.

Lucas provided Mike with a new envelope every day. Mike would come home excited to see what the day's assignment was. He was remembering things from his youth that he hadn't thought about in years and was beginning to see how they shaped where he found himself now.

After one week of deep work, the following week was a "break." During the break weeks, the assignments were centered around feeling the body, drawing, breath work, and long walks.

Mike had his first appointment with his therapist, Phil. He liked Phil and felt comfortable talking with him, and most importantly, he was honest with him. Mike had lived a lie for so long that being honest, even about small things, was a challenge for him.

This was one of Mike's biggest realizations in those early weeks. He lied about simple things—small things that didn't matter and big things that did. The realization was that he was constantly lying to himself. He made great effort to begin telling the truth.

The things we learned about Mike through this newfound truth-telling were unsettling. Mike had done some shady things when he was fueled up on alcohol and cocaine and a few prescription medications. It's no wonder that his life was in shambles. He had no respect for himself, and he was numb to his own emotions. That led to treating others in disrespectful, possibly harmful ways that he could not see at the time.

The second deep exercise week was centered around Mike's excessive shopping, the need for brand-name clothes, and expensive watches. Though centered around current behaviors, the writing brought up childhood memories that Mike had suppressed.

He discovered that the one he looked up to the most in his family was an uncle. This uncle was a bona fide loan shark, living on the darker side of legality. He was flashy, loud-mouthed, and a bully.

He dressed well, always had a Rolex watch, drove expensive cars, and seemed to young Mike to be the one in the family that had everything together.

This became Mike's idea of success. He craved his uncle's approval and attention, but that didn't come. His uncle told him outright that he thought Mike would never amount to anything and that he was weak.

In contrast to the uncle, Mike's father was a solid working man. They weren't rich and couldn't afford the brand-name clothes, but they were well taken care of.

To young Mike, that looked like failure when compared to the uncle.

With the memory of the uncle, Mike realized that the excessive shopping and obsession with brand names and expensive watches were just playing dress-up to look like young Mike's vision of success.

In reality, Mike was deeply in debt but sported a Rolex, drove a BMW and wore brand name clothes. This realization shook Mike to the core. It was a powerful thread that was pulled and with it came further unraveling.

Mike sold his watch.

With the memories of the uncle unearthed, Mike began remembering other things about those early years. The work was getting more challenging as these memories came up, and Mike started spending the afternoons in Lucas's office. He would write and then needed to speak about it. Lucas spent many hours listening and acting as a mirror for Mike while he was unraveling childhood assumptions.

Lucas describes this time as sitting as no one, having no thoughts, but somehow seeing through to the root of the issues with Mike. Words came out of Lucas that resonated strongly with Mike.

Lucas doesn't have much memory of these conversations; he was simply present, listening and responding when it felt indicated with words that simply came to and through him.

Mike had another suppressed memory. When he was 12, he got beaten up badly by a kid who lived in the neighborhood. He never told anyone. Lucas was the first person he had ever told. He realized that the reason he didn't tell anyone was because of his uncle's proclamation that he was weak.

In young Mike's mind, this had now been proven. He was weak, just like his uncle said. Mike suggested that this was the event that led to him completely shutting down his emotions. He was more determined than ever to act tough like his uncle, though he really believed he was weak on the inside. The character began to shape itself around the construct of a loan shark uncle's words.

When Mike had this memory, his body reacted. Mike started shaking, felt dizzy, and his breathing became fast and shallow. Lucas had Mike lie down on the floor and walked him through some breathing exercises. Mike's body was twitching, and he felt what he described as 'energy' shooting through him.

Lucas explained that while Mike may not have thought about the incident in years, the body remembered and had never let it go. It took about 20 minutes for Mike's body to let the energy flow through. Lucas sat with him through all of this, and when Mike got up, he said he felt lighter.

This is another great example of the body/mind conspiracy. The body keeps the secrets; it holds the narrative; the stories and emotions that we suppress are kept alive in the body. When our emotions are not allowed to fully process, they get stuck in incomplete expression.

Even if we don't remember the details of the story, the body does. Mike didn't think this story was of much importance; it happened when he was a young boy, and he thought he had let it go. The body told a different story.

This story was never let go by Mike; he had held onto it for 40+ years.

Mike was still seeing his therapist, Phil, once a week. Phil was helpful with things like leading Mike through guided meditations to relax and being a sounding board for the realizations Mike was having. It was helpful for Mike to have that outside perspective—a different perspective than Lucas and I had—and we encouraged Mike to continue to be honest and open with Phil about the things he was remembering and how they affected him.

Lucas and I are not therapists. We simply see how the Ego structure operates. That can make it difficult at times to 'meet people where they are' because most of Ego's manipulations are seen clearly, and it's important to remember that they are not seen at all by most people. Having a therapist was a necessity for Mike in our minds.

Once again, we fell into a rhythm in the household. Mike had his work scheduled out for him; he still insisted on doing the dishes every evening, and then Lucas and I would prepare dinner, and we would talk about his discoveries of the day.

Sometimes Mike would eat dinner with us, but most nights he took his plate to his room. This worked well for all of us, giving each of us some time and space outside of "Mike's Healing Journey."

Mike still cleaned but not obsessively like when he first arrived. He contributed in whatever ways he could. Sunday dinners were fun for him during this time. He would call his mom and get recipes for foods he liked as a kid. He would shop for the ingredients, time the cooking, and seemed to really enjoy that. It sometimes got away from him if the timing was complicated, but we were always there to lend a hand.

Mike was progressing and was excited about his own progress. He was unearthing a lot, and it almost became a new addiction for him. He discovered that he had been playing dress-up his entire life.

He didn't have any passions or hobbies of his own; they were all borrowed from other people. If others thought it was cool, then he would do it. He was emulating his uncle and, to some extent his cousin in Colombia. There was no 'Mike' on his own; his character relied solely on outside feedback, from the clothes he wore to the car he drove to the music he listened to.

Everything was for outside validation. This was why he never wore those shoes I said I didn't like and why he bought so many of the same shirt because I said I did like it. There was no "Mikeness" in Mike—only the appropriation of other people's tastes, beliefs and opinions.

This was why he seemed not to know anything about life or how to care for himself. He would follow us around the kitchen while we prepared dinner, trying to learn how to emulate cooking—not learning how to cook, but learning how to act like he knew how to cook. He would also follow us around whenever we were doing chores around the house; he needed constant input. This is why he had to tell us every time he cleaned something. It was very much like the "Look at me, Mommy!" stage of a child.

He didn't have any internal character; it was all propped up from the outside.

Over the next several weeks, the work grew deeper. It covered self-image, family relationships, and then went into romantic relationships. There were days when Mike would come down for dinner, and his entire head and neck were bright red. He would say he felt like his brain was on fire.

He was unraveling things at a rapid pace. We insisted that he take breaks when it got like this. He was moving too fast for reality to reframe around the character's deconstruction. He would take a break for a week, talk to Phil, go on long walks, and regain some sense of calm.

When working with Mike through these things, we had to introduce language to communicate the Ego structure and Ego character in layman's terms to give Mike an understanding of what was happening.

We used the symbology of Maya, the goddess of illusion, to give him some separation between the "I" and the thoughts that were running through his head. This seemed to make sense to Mike and gave him a visual to make the distinction between what was *actually happening* and the thoughts *about* what was happening. This seemed to help him.

He began dissecting the thoughts and seeing the Ego character mechanics at work. When he began feeling anxious, he would use the visual of Maya, and he was able to calm the thoughts and not be controlled by them.

Mike was doing well at this stage. He had made some friends in rehab and would occasionally go to dinner with them. He still had contact with a couple that he knew from the "old days" and would visit them.

He attended a couple of social events where drinking was happening, but he felt no urge to participate. He had a newfound understanding of how it affected him and his decision-making, and he didn't want to go down that road again. He was rebuilding social connections and having some enjoyable times.

This was important because the intensity of the work he was doing with Lucas required the counterbalance of remembering that life was still going on and was enjoyable.

The unmasking that Mike was doing is something that few people have the courage to do. He kept going through many Fracture Points, through heart palpitations and anxious moments that this level of work brings on. There were days he wanted to quit, when it felt like too much, and we encouraged him to take necessary breaks.

Mike did not quit. As weak as he believed he was, he was courageous enough to walk into his own black hole time and time again. Most folks would have quit after the first mask that fractured their worldview was revealed. Mike didn't. He kept exposing the masks.

Both Lucas and I had incredible respect for Mike and his willingness to keep going further.

Mike got to the point of realizing that there really was no Mike. He understood conceptually that it was all just thoughts, made up as he went.

He would say, "I don't know who I am anymore. I don't know what I like or what I don't like; I don't know anything at all." He would continue, "It's like there's nothing inside; there's no Me. I borrowed my life from a bunch of other people." This is a hard pill for anyone to swallow. Mike naturally had some ups and downs about this.

It's important to understand that Mike knew this conceptually, but he was NOT experiencing "no self." This was not collapse. This wasn't yet Rupture; it was the result of many Fracture Points. It was simply an understanding of how the character had organized itself around the perception of other people's opinions and preferences, always seeking outside validation.

Lucas and I would joke with him about it. "Do you know how much money and countless hours in meditation have been spent trying to understand the concept that there is no 'me'? And you got it for free!"

As Mike kept going, exposing his Ego character, Ego struck back. This is how it operates. The structure will move in to try to repair the Fracture Points. It will morph into whatever it needs to be to keep the illusion of itself as a separate entity intact.

When Mike got the understanding of "no real me", Ego Protective Services stepped in to correct the situation.

Mike made a U-turn from the "I don't know who I am" realization and began viewing it through the lens of "I have realized that who I thought I was before was all made-up, but now I can become someone real with more advanced knowledge than others."

Mike began using the 'Maya' symbolism in his everyday speech. He would speak in the terms that Lucas and I would use to try to explain the structure to him. He soon sounded very wise and articulated the ideas well.

What we were watching happen in real time was the Ego appropriating a new language and new concepts and constructing a new identity to replace the unraveling of the old one.

Once again, Mike began coming home from the outpatient rehab sessions saying that he was so much more advanced than those other people.

He would say things like, "Working with you guys has giving me a much deeper understanding and I feel like everyone else, is just dealing with surface bullshit, child's play."

He began to feel that way about his therapist, Phil, as well. We called this out to him, explaining that this is one of the many weapons that Ego uses. He was simply reconstructing the character into one that was more advanced than others, one that was deep and doing the really hard work of healing.

Mike was also having physical sensations to go along with this newfound identity. He shared with us that he sometimes felt like he was floating. Sometimes he felt like he was outside of his body and watching himself.

He had amazing energy sensations in his body. He felt like he was "vibrating with life," as he described it. He just knew that something very profound was happening to him.

This is not so different from the spiritual seekers with their ideas on Kundalini awakening or out-of-body experiences or feeling the energy in the body and creating a narrative that their 'light body' is activating.

These things feel profound, and we put some fun, exciting, mystical labels on them. Most of the time, it's simply the nervous system readjusting and reformatting. But that doesn't sound sexy, mystical, or lend the Ego the importance it craves.

With this character emerging, Mike thought it was time for him to go back to his business and reconnect with his family. He thought he had learned so much and that he was ready.

He made a plan to go to the business to talk to his oldest son, Alex, who was working there. Lucas and I strongly discouraged this. We told him that Alex might feel ambushed and that there was no way of knowing if he wanted to talk to him at all at this point. There had been no contact.

The last attempted contact was when Mike returned from Colombia. He wrote an email to his family explaining that he had relapsed but that he was returning to rehab and committed to getting better. There had been no reply to that email. Mike was adamant that he needed to reach out to Alex.

Lucas offered a compromise. He would go with Mike and talk to Alex first. If that went well and Alex wanted to talk to Mike, then Lucas would give him the all-clear.

Mike got very anxious when the day came. We had not seen that level of anxiety in him to date. Lucas drove him over to the business and went in. Alex was working, and there were no customers at that time, so they had a moment alone to talk.

Lucas told Alex that his dad would really like to see him, but that we didn't know how Alex felt about it. Alex really opened up to Lucas.

The family assumed that Mike was just living with us, continuing to drink, and that we were just partying with our friend every night. Lucas was able to set the record straight on what was happening in our house. He told him that Mike was working really hard to get better, harder than most people ever attempt.

Alex brought up Colombia and Marisol and Lucas told him that Mike had cut off contact with her and was committed to his rehab work.

Alex told Lucas that Clark and Martha had encouraged the family to go to Al-Anon, and they were attending those meetings regularly and going to a Christian church. Al-Anon was adamant that there should be "no contact" with the addict, and Clark and Martha had forbidden them to contact Mike, so they were abiding by that "rule."

Clark and Martha had also taken over the business, opened a new LLC, and were operating the business that Mike had built under the same name, with a new bank account using Mike's equipment, his customers, and his inventory.

Lucas informed Alex that those actions amounted to fraud and theft. Alex looked ashen and said, "Do you think he'll sue us?" "They just did it so he wouldn't take the money."

Lucas replied, "That's not my call; I imagine he could sue you—something to be aware of. At the very least, these actions were dishonest and in bad faith. They've stolen a business. That would be like walking into your mechanic's shop, sending him on vacation, and when he comes back, the shop has the same name but someone else is profiting from the customers, the tools, and the machinery. I'm not sure I would be comfortable making a living that way."

Alex shared with Lucas that not only did they not want Mike to take money from the business, but that Clark and Martha were also only giving Naomi a monthly allowance. Alex said, "She's not really good with money, so it's working out."

It was pretty disturbing how much influence and control Clark and Martha had over this family.

At the end of the conversation, Alex held firm to his belief in Al-Anon and no contact. He didn't think he should see or speak to his dad.

He was glad that Mike was doing the work to get better and not drinking, and he was comforted to know that it wasn't just a 24/7 party at our house, but he wasn't ready to have contact.

He said if Mike came back to the business, he wouldn't work there with him.

Lucas gave the news to Mike. The disappointment was crushing. The betrayal by Clark and Martha was new information. He had thought that they cared about him. At the end of the day, they had deceived him about their intentions, and he realized that none of this was done out of concern for him.

These folks had hijacked his family and his business.

When Mike and Lucas got home, we sat out in the backyard so Lucas could tell me about the conversation with Alex. When he got to the part about telling Alex that Mike had cut off all contact with Marisol, there was a flicker of something in Mike's reaction that immediately registered—Mike had lied about cutting off contact.

Lucas caught it too. Neither of us said anything to Mike, the day was tough enough for him already.

Lucas and I discussed it after Mike went to his room. We both had the same suspicion that Mike had not cut off contact with Marisol. The day was Friday. The work coming up for Mike on Monday was about romantic relationships.

On Sunday, we broached the subject. I said, "So this coming week is about relationships. Would you agree that you have a relationship with us?" Mike agreed and said that the relationship with us was the most honest relationship he had ever had.

I responded, "Honesty, yes. That's what's needed for relationships to thrive. In light of that, both Lucas and I feel like there may be some lingering dishonesty surrounding Marisol." Mike paled and said "How did you know?"

It turns out that while Mike did indeed delete her pictures and her number from his phone and laptop, he had another phone hidden and had been in daily contact with her the entire time. In Mike's mind, it wasn't really a lie because he did delete things off the devices we knew about.

Mike almost seemed relieved that we found out. He told us that he felt terrible keeping it from us, and the worst part was that he couldn't talk to us about the things he was dealing with. The relationship was wearing on him; the more he untangled about himself, the more he was seeing that this was just another addiction.

He then shared that he had planned to go to the UK to visit his mom. Originally, he made this plan to get out from under our watchful eyes.

He was going to see his mom but then tell us he was coming back on a date 14 days after he actually flew in; he was going to land and immediately board a flight to Colombia, thinking we wouldn't find out. He freely admitted this, saying, "This is how devious my mind is." As much as he felt bad, his character got a real payoff from feeling like he was getting away with something.

At some point between making this plan and the day it all came out, something had clicked, and he wasn't so enamored with Marisol any longer. He actually did cut off all contact that day.

These two events, his son not wanting to speak to him and cutting off contact with Marisol, were the beginning of Rupture for Mike. The cracks were widening.

The Monday after cutting off Marisol, Mike woke up in a depressed mood. There had been up days and down days through this entire time, but he was generally able to pull out of the bad days and keep going. This day was different.

He had to drag himself to rehab; he came home and told us he felt anxious. He wasn't in the mood to talk to anyone at rehab and couldn't wait to get back home where he was "safe." This was a little puzzling to us, but we talked it through with him. Lucas did some breathing exercises with him, and by evening he felt better.

The next morning, he was afraid to leave the house. We talked it through, and he made it to rehab and back but then needed a long nap. The next day was the same. We thought perhaps this was some aftereffects of letting go of his last pacifier, Marisol.

When we shared this with Mike, he agreed and thought that it was likely. Having a reason seemed to release anxiety's grip on him.

Thursday morning came, and Mike was incredibly upbeat. He would be graduating from rehab again that day. He dressed up, he left the house feeling like a million bucks, and when he came home, he was flying high.

He had the best day! He was engaging with folks like the "old Mike" could, chatting up a storm with strangers. He was joyful; he was positive about life and what the future would hold.

Mike was still scared about dealing with the drama of ending the marriage and untangling the business, but it was a fear he was ready to face. He realized that by leaving it all hanging out there, it was dead weight that would cling to him until he got it resolved.

He asked for our help with this next phase, and we gladly agreed. We told him that we were willing to help him and support him through the divorce process and with whatever he wanted to do with his business. Mike was adamant about fighting for his business but wanted to make sure that his family was properly looked after throughout the entire process. He felt he owed them that.

That evening, with this glowing feeling of positivity, Mike wrote an email to Clark and Martha. He wrote that it was time for him to take responsibility for his business and his life and that he needed some information about the business so he could deal with some financial decisions that needed to be made.

The business had some debt, and he needed to understand how that was being paid with this new setup. The email was strong, decisive, and professional. He wanted to work with them to handle things, tie up loose ends, and find the best resolution for all involved.

He felt elated when he pressed "SEND."

That was the last time we saw any resemblance of our friend Mike.

Friday morning came, and Mike slept in. He didn't have to go to rehab, so he took the day off. We didn't see much of him that day, he was in his room or out for walks while we were working.

By that evening, the light had left his eyes. He was down, anxious, and fidgety. He wasn't talkative; he just sat in the living room chair and stared into space. When we asked if he was ok, he simply said, "Yeah, I'm fine. Just tired."

Saturday came, and it was more of the same but with a little more anxiety. Saturday evening, Mike came and told us that he wouldn't be able to handle dinner on Sunday. He just didn't feel like he could manage the shopping and the preparation.

Concerned, we pressed him to tell us what was really going on. He told us he got a response to his email; he pulled it up and let us read it. The email was devastating to Mike.

Clark and Martha had responded again, speaking for the entire family. They told him that he had not been sober long enough to be involved with any of them. No mention was made of how long would be long enough.

It went on to say there was nothing to discuss about the business because it was operating under a new entity. The old business debt was Mike's problem. They wanted no contact, no involvement. If he tried to come into the business, they would contact the authorities and get a restraining order.

They implied that by trying to have contact with his children, he was harming them and hampering them from moving on with life, and if he loved them at all, he would leave them alone.

The language of the letter was spiteful and threatening, throwing every failure back in Mike's face.

It was clear to us that Clark and Martha had never had any intention of turning the business back over to Mike. They stole it and were profiting from it. They were also controlling the money that Naomi was "allowed" to have from it.

This couple, who claimed to be his friends, looking out for his and his family's best interests, were nothing more than opportunists. They were playing out their "savior" roles, justifying their deceitful actions by claiming to be taking care of the family.

I think this betrayal was as impactful as the family not wanting to have contact with Mike.

This was full-on Rupture.

All this time, Mike had been operating under the assumption that if he got clean and sober and did the work to get his life back in order, his family and friends would be there for him.

He was now left with the knowledge that there was nothing he could do. No amount of work, no length of sobriety, and no getting himself together would be enough to have a relationship with his family.

He also realized that Clark and Martha cared nothing for him; they were the saviors of his wife and children in their minds. Mike now realized that he had nothing.

His entire sham of a life was demolished in one fell swoop.

Over the next week, the anxiety grew worse. Mike wouldn't leave the house; he didn't feel safe "out there."

We did our best to talk to him, listen to him, and work through relaxation techniques with him. That helped during the day, but then when night fell and we went to bed, it would all come back.

The anxiety appeared as pacing, fidgeting, picking at his fingernails, constant movement in his body. He couldn't sleep; he lost his appetite. He needed constant companionship. He would sit in Lucas's office while he was working just to be near him; he couldn't be alone.

We tried some natural remedies with him, like magnesium and lavender. Mike was used to taking pills that did something immediately; he had no patience for natural things to work.

He wanted it fixed NOW.

Depression and suicidal ideation also showed up. He would say, "I just want to go to sleep and never wake up," and "I can't believe this has happened to me."

The following Saturday morning, Mike came down and said that he thought he needed to go to the hospital and get some medication because the anxiety was full-blown and he couldn't stop it.

I told him that if that's what he thought he needed, we would support that, but since he had suicidal thoughts, we couldn't in good faith let him go up to his room with a bottle full of pills that would do the job. If they gave him a prescription, he would need to give it to us, and we would make sure he took the dosage correctly until he felt more in control and could handle it on his own. He agreed to that, and Lucas took him to the emergency room.

The hospital here is still working under Covid protocols, so no one is allowed in the emergency room with you. Lucas made sure he got in, stayed in the parking lot until Mike sent a text that he had been taken to a room. Lucas came back home and told Mike to call when he was ready, and he would go pick him up. The hospital is about a 15-minute drive away.

At the emergency room, they did the regular physical assessments to make sure he wasn't having a heart attack or a stroke, and then they conducted a psychiatric evaluation. He told them that yes, he had suicidal thoughts. Then they asked him if he had started planning *how* to end his life.

The answer to this ridiculous question is apparently the ultimate litmus test for whether you need serious mental health treatment or if you just need some pills. Mike said he had not planned the *how*, and so this was enough for them to simply send him home with a couple of prescriptions.

They gave him six Xanax pills to take home and a prescription for a six-month supply, along with the same six-month prescription for Lexapro. No mental health counseling was required. In my mind, this was a great example of the joke that "healthcare" has become.

They prescribed a suicidal, recovering addict a six-month supply of Xanax without a second thought.

After several hours, Lucas sent a text and Mike answered that he would just take an Uber home. When he got home, it was a different Mike that walked in.

He was petulant like a child. He threw the Xanax bottle down on the table and said, "There, see? They only gave me six pills, not much I can do with that. Are you satisfied that you don't have to treat me like a child now?" He then informed us that he was going to stay over at some friends' house for the night and he left.

The next morning, Mike came home at around 10 a.m. He came in, sat down, and apologized. "I'm sorry for how I acted. I realize that I got myself all worked up just to get the pills. It's the only thing that gives me relief from the racing thoughts, and I just wanted a break." "I know you aren't big on medication, and I felt like I let you down." "I talked about it with my friends, and they think I need to be on medication long-term."

I was a little taken aback by his feeling of letting us down or that medication was a failure. "Mike, I'm not against medication. It's a tool in the toolbox. I had a horrible experience with medication in my younger years when I was struggling with depression, so I don't utilize medications of any kind for the most part anymore.

Because of that, I don't know what medication is even out there anymore; it's not a world that I live in, but it is a tool in the toolbox that might be of help to you." I continued, "There is no such thing as letting us down; this is not about us, we don't matter. What matters is that you get what you need.

If you have a broken leg, then a crutch is necessary while the leg heals; the same could be said for anti-anxiety medication."

This seemed to relieve him. He then said he didn't want to have to take pills for the rest of his life and that he really wanted to work it out without them. I said it was his choice, but we needed to be smart about how we use the tools and to make sure that Phil, his therapist, knows about this so he can help monitor the situation.

Unfortunately, the pills didn't do much for Mike. The anxiety continued to rage. He stopped leaving the house, would go days without showering, and was sinking deeper into the abyss of nihilism.

Nothing mattered; he just wanted to go to sleep and never wake up. He had nothing to live for; he was a sham, and pills were a crutch. He still could not come to terms with the reality of the situation.

He lost everything, was defaulting on debt that might have legal consequences down the line, and had no self-preservation instinct. He was fully in the grasp of hopelessness.

We still talked with him each day, sometimes for hours. Every conversation came back to "I can't believe this happened and I won't get over it." Once again, Ego was restructuring itself, this time into a victim identity.

We cautioned him over and over again about this stage. When this identity is allowed to solidify, it becomes much harder to get out of it.

This victim identity takes over every thought and the functioning of the body. This is the Ego in full-on resistance. It hardens like concrete and takes a lot to crack it. It gives itself away in the language, though. "I can't and I won't." "I won't" being the largest obstacle.

When the victim identity runs its thought loops, it becomes "I won't get over this." This becomes the anthem; the soundtrack underlying every thought. It also prophesies the outcome if left unchecked. It's Ego's fiction of volition, "I WON'T".

We pointed this out to Mike several times. "You CAN get over this, but not if you're identifying with the thought loop of **I won't**. You are choosing to stay exactly where you are.

You believe you deserve the punishment, and what better way to punish yourself?" "The question is, when is it enough? When will the self-punishment be enough?"

Mike would understand this conceptually; however, the loop pulled him back in time and time again.

To the Ego, doing everything it can to maintain its false identity, nothing is off-limits. It would rather exist as the self-punishing voice in the head than not at all.

Mike, who was once dismantling his identification with thought loops, seeing clearly that who he thought he was was a fictional construct built over years, was now identifying *as* victim and as victim thoughts.

The simulation struck back, in a big way.

Mike's therapist was clearly out of his depth as well. The last piece of advice he gave Mike was to go home and see his mom; that the change of location may very well fix everything. Mike even saw through this. He stated that he knew changing location wouldn't fix anything because he would be taking 'him' to the new place.

Phil really shit the bed on this one, but he was most likely grasping at straws. What he had witnessed in the deconstruction of Mike through these weeks was not something he was trained for or had any knowledge of. I'm sure he did his best.

As the weeks drew out, all Mike did was ruminate in his thoughts. Every day was the same. Mike would come down to sit and repeat the same story. "I can't believe this has happened to me. I wish I could do something to change what happened. I don't know what to do. I just want to go to sleep and never wake up."

One evening, Mike was sitting outside with us. He hadn't showered in a few days, and he was playing this story on repeat once again. I said, "Mike, you can't change what happened. All you can do is deal with what is and move from there."

He replied, "I can't accept what is; I just wish there was something I could do to change it." I said, "Well, shit in one hand and wish in the other and see which one fills up first." This snapped Mike out of the loop for a moment. This was not the reaction, sympathy, pity, or feedback that he was going for.

I continued, "Understand, Mike, this has already happened; there is nothing you can do to make it *not* have happened. What you *can* do is deal with right now, and one great way to do that would be to take a shower. Sitting around in your own filth isn't going to make anything better."

"Deal with right now, the needs of the moment. Shower, make your bed, brush your teeth. Write, get the thought loops out of your head where you can look at them. You know that works for you; you've just given up trying."

Mike was taken aback. He was looking for commiseration, not straight talk. The Victim Character immediately responded with, "It's pretty hard to do when you don't even want to live. I just want to go to sleep and never wake up."

I was very familiar with this character; I was in the deep pit of suicidal depression in my twenties, and I recognized this reaction.

It's a defense that is just so over-the-top that no one will dare to penetrate it. I penetrated.

I responded, "OK, go pack a bag." Shocked, Mike said, "What for?" I said, "Well, you're technically under our care, and you've just said you want to kill yourself. As responsible adults, we have a duty to take you to the nearest mental health facility and check you in because you are threatening self-harm."

Mike was stunned. This is not what he was expecting. He immediately toned the rhetoric down. "I'm not going to do anything; it's just how I feel at the moment." I replied, "Yes, you keep saying that you don't want to wake up and you think about killing yourself, but how do you know that will solve it?

Do you know what happens when you kill the body? What if the mind survives? Then you're really up the creek. For someone who is completely afraid to leave the house, who is afraid of life, you sure seem comfortable with the great unknown of death.

Tell me, Mike, are you afraid of death?" He could not believe that this defense of all defenses was being challenged. It interrupted the groove of the thought loop.

He replied, "Yes, I'm afraid of death; everyone is. I don't really want to die; I just don't know what to do." I nodded and said, "I thought so. May we agree that causing your own death is complete rubbish and off the table? We can't really move on if we've convinced ourselves that suicide is a viable option. It isn't really anything you want to do; showering is a challenge for you right now; the planning and execution of a successful suicide doesn't seem likely at this point."

Mike laughed and agreed. I said, "it's just a little fantasy that digs the pit of the victim a little deeper." Mike nodded and said, "I know; I can see that." I added, "I'm not making light of suicide or the thoughts surrounding it, Mike. If that's really where your action plan is taking you, then we need to get you into a mental health facility immediately; you understand that, right?"

He said, "I'm not going to kill myself, you're right, I know it's just the loopy thoughts, I just don't know how to stop them at the moment. Right now, I think I'll go take a shower."

It's important to note on particularly challenging days for Mike, we were watchful in case the suicidal thoughts were taking a stronger hold. If he began that line of conversation, we would suggest that it was time to go to a mental health facility. He always refused. Mike knew that it was a defense mechanism.

We talked openly about suicide and the thoughts around it, taking some of the air out of that thought balloon.

Side Note: The understanding of my struggle with the suicide loop in my youth is this:

I had experienced a complete Rupture at the time. As everything that I had thought was important, real, or had meaning was stripped away, I was seeing through the illusion of meaning, self, importance, striving, and relationships.

I had no language for it at the time. There was a deep inner knowing that there actually was no point to any of it. Without any guideposts for what was happening, it simply felt like the best solution was to go to sleep and never wake up. I'm familiar with this thought process.

What I see now is that the one who needed meaning and purpose, the character, was the one that eventually sought out pills. The one that needed to reintegrate into the dream so that it had meaning again was the structure repairing itself so that the show would go on.

This experience and understanding are what make this character comfortable talking about suicide and penetrating that defense mechanism.

I don't make light of it; I simply question it from different angles until we can get to the bottom of what's really happening and deal with that.

That is what we did with Mike: questioned every single angle of the thought loop every time.

On days when he worked himself up into a frenzy of anxiety, frustrated that the pills weren't working and convincing himself he would be like this forever, we would also suggest that perhaps he needed some in-patient mental health care.

Each time, Mike magically got hold of himself. He did not want to get into the mental health industrial complex.

Mike conceptually understood that nothing from the outside was going to help him; he also understood that most of his story on repeat was reaching for sympathy, to validate the victim character.

He felt that if he went to in-patient care, he would most likely be sedated even more, and he didn't want that. He didn't see how further medicating himself would help him; he just viewed it as a crutch.

He would say, "I went through all of this to deal with my addictions, only to be told that I'll need pills for the rest of my life? What a f@cking joke."

Through our many hours spent talking with Mike during this stage, it was interesting to note that Mike absolutely understood what was happening to him conceptually. He knew that "he" was choosing to stay in victimhood and hopelessness. He admitted that several times.

I asked him one day if he thought that staying in this stage wasn't so much about punishing himself, but punishing Clark, Martha, and the family—something along the lines of "See what you've done to me now?"

He thought about that for a few minutes. When he looked up, he made very direct eye contact with me and said "Yes."

That look felt like I was seeing the Ego structure directly, not the fuzzy character. It was something in the look, the way he answered.

The weeks dragged on. Some days were better than others. Mike understood that no one could get him out of this abyss but him. He was the only one who could continue to challenge the thoughts in his head. He knew he had to find the will to fight his own way out of this stage; he just couldn't find it.

He simply kept repeating, "I can't believe this has happened to me."

Denial and victimhood had settled in, and they weren't going to leave any time soon. He wore them like an old familiar blanket. Some days he would forget that this was his identity now and catch himself in a joke or a smile, and it would shut down immediately.

A smile or a joke was not consistent with the damaged, depressed, victim character. When anything not consistent with this character would sneak out, the Ego structure emergency services crew would respond immediately to put the fire out.

Part of the issue was, I think, that Mike's entire identity from childhood was held up from the outside. He wasn't one of those folks who built the character from the inside. It depended entirely on outside validation for its existence.

There would have been no jumping-off point for him to understand that the key to busting through this phase could be found on the inside.

After some time, Mike decided he needed to visit his mom in the UK; that maybe it would help him in some way.

I also think the sympathy train had run out of track with us and he wasn't getting the outside validation that the victim character needed. He was getting an ass-kicking mixed in with understanding, but he was not getting sympathy, pity, or validation from us.

The anxiety turned up a notch that entire week before his departure. How was he going to get on a plane when he couldn't even leave the house?

The morning of the flight was over the top. We told him to use the tools in the toolbox, take half a Xanax, pack your things, take another half before we go to the airport. We'll walk you in and make sure you get checked in. We held his hand through the entire thing. The Xanax did its job, and he was able to check in and felt calm enough to go through security.

When he hugged us goodbye, we knew he was saying "goodbye," not "see you later." "He held us both tightly, thanked us for all we had done for him with a promise that he would pay us back someday.

We were all holding back tears, it was incredibly emotional. When he went up the stairs toward security, he waived like a little kid, and we waived back in the same manner.

We had a text conversation with him as he was waiting for the plane to board; he was doing okay and felt confident that the flight would go smoothly.

We got another text when he landed and then when he arrived at his mom's house.

It was four months before we heard from him again. He called us saying that he was really unhappy in the UK and thought the best thing for him was to come back.

"At least there, I was somebody, I was the Brit making my way in America. Here, I'm just another person." The Ego structure was grasping for anything to repair itself.

We reminded him that location was not the issue. For various reasons, it was not a good idea for Mike to return. Listening to him build his case, it became clear that he had a new fantasy world in his head that looked something like this: He would return, his wife and children would forgive him, he would take the business back over, and life would be back to "normal."

We walked him through all the faulty reasoning, encouraged him to continue to write, and continue to see his therapist regularly, but most of all, we encouraged him once again to simply look around and accept what IS. Mike told us he still could not accept it.

When Mike left, he left most of his things in his room, we had to clean it out. He left his BMW, it was repossessed. There is nothing left here for him: a shattered life, massive debt, and an estranged family. He was still living in denial, clinging to the victim identity and refusing to accept the reality of the present.

After another eight months had passed, we got an email from Mike.

He had finally come to terms with what had happened, and he found what he needed to crawl out of the pit of despair he had kept himself in.

He was slowly engaging in life again—getting up early, going on long morning walks, working in the garden, and even had a part time job at the local hardware store.

It was a short email, but he wanted us to know that he didn't quit. He still felt like he was hanging by a thread some days, but those were getting fewer and farther between and he was finding joy in the simple life he was leading. He said it started turning around when he finally, simply accepted the situation.

The structure repaired as much as it could of the Rupture; the character found another identity in the simple life.

He still hasn't spoken to his kids, but he's come to terms with that.

Mike got back up after a tremendous fall. His experience of life will never be the same. He has a new perspective. A new story. Rupture was repaired but Collapse didn't come. Mike has seen the illusion of Self, this was the cause of the anxiety. It lasted until the repair process completed.

The story of Mike continues, but with lower-budget stage props and much less destructive drama.

This story is cautionary for a few reasons:

It details how the Ego character/structure and simulation will resist with weapons you can't imagine when Rupture happens. When the structure is weakened, sometimes the only repair is taking on a new identity, even if it's a miserable one. This is why the warnings in this book and in the Lenswork Workbook are there. This work is not to be taken lightly.

It shows how fake awakening works when the Ego appropriates a more enlightened, wiser language and identity.

It shows how not to treat people going through rehab. Clark and Martha had a big part in destroying a life simply because they were playing out their own character identification as saviors. The situation may have been a little different had there been any real concern for Mike as a person and the possible reasons why addiction took over his life. But there wasn't. In simulation, there are always victims and villains, and often, people play both parts.

We'll be revisiting some of the stages of this story as we continue with the rest of the book and explain in detail the functions of the simulation mechanics that were at work.

FAKE AWAKE
AMBIEN SLEEPWALKERS SELLING YOU A DREAM OF AWAKENING

Before we dive into this book, it's important to define what we mean by **"Awakening."** This is a word that has been overused, and it means different things to different people.

First off, we need to make it clear that we will be steering clear of the word **"Spiritual"** as it relates to awakening. The term spiritual is extremely subjective and misleading. This term can lead our minds to relate it to a plethora of beliefs about souls, higher powers, religious figures, dimensions of existence, frequency or vibration, and a host of other notions.

The term **'Spiritual'** has simply become the overarching brand of all belief systems that we find in the Spiritual Industrial Complex, and because it is so closely related to belief, it is no longer a useful term. Let's clear some things up:

> Awakening is **not** Spiritual.
> Awakening is **not** personal.
> Awakening **cannot** be achieved.
> Awakening does **not** have a path.

Regardless of what you may have been sold, most of what gets called awakening today is just a costume change. The actor is still the same. The lighting is warmer, the wardrobe is more relaxed, and the words are chosen to sound deep.

But under the surface, it is the same character with the same habits and the same obsession with staying in the spotlight.

Here are a few examples of the best-selling awaking products:

Ascension from 3D to 5D and beyond, becoming a lightworker, having contact with the galactic federation, raising your frequency or vibration, experiencing psychedelic oneness, ayahuasca ceremonies, ashram experiences, workshops on creating your reality, balancing your karma, escaping the reincarnation loop, cancelling your soul contracts, reclaiming lost parts of your soul, past life regression, kundalini, some yoga practices, prolonged meditative states, catching it like a virus from sitting at the feet of a guru, the dark night of the soul, shadow work, activating your DNA, channeling the central sun to activate your light body, gaining insight into the lies and propaganda of the media, becoming an expert on conspiracy theories, Ego death – the path to eternal bliss, awakening journeys complete with 'stages of awakening' to track your progress.

This list could go on and on and on in several run-on sentences that are equally as hard to read as the last one.

These are NOT awakening. Some of these experiences may be part of the **Arc of Awakening,** but the experiences themselves are not awakening.

All that has happened is the character has safely pressed the snooze button and rolled back over into a deeper sleep but with better dreams.

These are **FAKE AWAKE.**

Much like folks who take Ambien are prone to sleepwalking, what the Spiritual Industrial Complex has sold as 'awakening' amounts to nothing more than Ambien Sleepwalkers selling books and courses on how to wake up.

When we reference the **Arc of Awakening,** it is not a path. It's simply function. There may be Fracture Points in life that immediately repair and add to the Ego's story. Some mystical experiences fall into this category.

An experience of psychedelic 'oneness' may be a Fracture Point. A fracture in the structure of your perceived reality. The structure repairs, and you go on with a new story of 'my experience of oneness.'

There may be so many Fracture Points that they result in Rupture. Rupture is harder to repair, but repair still happens.

An example would be losing your spouse, then your job, then getting your arm cut off in a horrific accident and getting a message in your head from Archangel Michael telling you that you had to go through all of this because you're a Chosen One.

These combined fractures could result in Rupture of your entire identity and perceived reality. These generally repair, restructuring into a new identity. In this case, the 'chosen one' with a universal mission identity.

Neither of these examples are awakening.

You can dedicate years to the spiritual grind. Wake up before dawn to meditate. Chant until your tongue goes numb. Sit in the presence of people who claim to be awake. You might even rack up some blissful moments or visions that feel like you have stepped outside of time. They might feel important, life-changing even. They are not awakening. They are spiritual postcards you send to yourself.

Awakening is not an achievement you earn like a medal for effort. It is not a new identity you put on like a fresh shirt.

It is not an experience you can keep in your pocket for when you need to feel special. It is not a place you arrive at. There is nowhere to arrive.

It is not about light or love or bliss or some magic frequency you can measure. Those things might show up, just like rain might show up on any given day. They don't define the weather, and they don't define awakening.

You cannot turn it into a lifestyle. You cannot buy the right clothes, move to the right city, drink the right tea, and call yourself awakened.

The Spiritual Industrial Complex will gladly sell you a brand called "awakening" and dress it up in retreats, incense, and carefully worded posts.

The moment it becomes something to display, you are back in the game and the game is the illusion.

If you came here looking for a set of instructions, that is not what this is. There is a workbook that exists for dismantling the supports that keep the Self in place. That is a tool for exposure.

This is not a tool. This is demolition.

This is the book you open when you are done pretending there are parts of the illusion worth saving.

Awakening is not what you think. In fact, it is not even yours. It is what remains when the one who was trying to get it is gone.

And if that feels disappointing, it is only because you still believe you are the kind of person who needs to feel good about the ending.

Interruption:

Stop. Before you go further, notice what is reading this. If you just felt interest or anticipation or recognition, that is the Self, saving itself a front row seat at its own funeral. This book is not for "you." If you continue, you do so knowing, that even the one turning the pages is a lie. Watch that lie while you read.

THE GREAT DISTORTION
EVERYTHING YOU THINK YOU SEE IS BACKWARDS

If you believed the marketing, awakening would sound like the ultimate lifestyle upgrade. Just a few inner shifts, some positive affirmations, a retreat or two, and you could be your most "Authentic Self" while keeping the Self completely intact.

Picture it: you're on a cliff at sunrise, posting a serene meditation photo with #alignment and #blessed, checking later to see how many people noticed your peace. This is the modern Spiritual Industrial Complex. It doesn't want the end of you. It wants a calmer, shinier, more photogenic you.

It sells awakening the same way it sells skin cream: *there's always another product, another layer to peel back, another transformation to buy.* The transaction is simple; you give them money, they give you permission to keep being you, just rebranded.

"Fake Awake" is not a rare problem, it's presented all over Social Media today. It is the default. The same Self gets recycled through gentler vocabulary. The person who once chased status now chases presence. The one obsessed with being right now wants to be wise. The one who sought enlightenment now claims it by identifying as the observer. The doormat personality with poor boundaries now has a universal mission as a lightworker. The addict recovers by adopting a new addiction to wellness. The costumes change, but the actor never leaves the stage.

The props are endless. Healing journeys that never end. Energy work to "raise your vibration" like a rechargeable battery. Shadow work so bottomless you never run out of Self to fix.

Meditation retreats that are so effective, you need another one within three weeks. Manifesting certification courses so you can pay for tracking just how far you've come in your manifesting journey.

Shamanic retreats that use psychedelics so you can vomit out your 'old self.' Body work retreats that teach that your fascia is the KEY to activating your light body.

Workshops on how to properly smudge evil spirits from your sacred space. Big, flashy Spiritual Expos that feature all of the above and MORE, complete with presentations from the "Super Spiritual Celebrities" as seen on your favorite talk shows!

There is something for every Self looking to level up their Selfhood.

✦ REMEMBER MIKE ✦

When Mike walked out of rehab the first time, he thought thirty days had remade him. He told himself he was stronger now, wiser, finally free. He wore the wristband like a badge of honor. To him, it was proof of transformation.

But distortion always inverts reality. What felt like awakening was just another costume. He wasn't healed, he was rehearsed. He had memorized the language, learned the posture, played the part. Fake awake.

Within weeks, he was drinking again. Yet he clung to the illusion: *That wasn't failure, it was part of my growth.* Each relapse became a distorted victory, proof (to him) that he was "learning."

Mike's story shows the Great Distortion at work: when decay masquerades as progress, when Rupture looks like strength, when relapse is renamed "lesson." Distortion flips the compass until down feels like up.

Remember Mike: the more convinced you are that you've changed, the more dangerous the distortion becomes.

These programs, marketing gimmicks, and beliefs are simply simulation at its most sophisticated, dismantling 'you' so you can rebuild into a better 'you.'

Yes, simulation. Not in the sci-fi "trapped in a computer" sense, but in the way a magic trick is a simulation: convincing, immersive, and running on hidden mechanics. If you look closely, you'll see the seams and the scaffolding holding it all up.

And yes, it feels like progress. You feel lighter, kinder, more "aligned." But the Self is still narrating, still starring in its own awakening story. You can tell because you keep checking how far along you are.

Interruption:

Right now, you may be silently agreeing. "Yes, I see this too." That agreement is ownership, the very thing this book is here to erase. This is not about you *seeing* the problem. This is about you *being* the problem and not surviving the exposure.

The illusion of progress is the sweetest trap. You can master every method, read every book, speak with the calm cadence of someone who meditates twice a day, and still never take one step closer to the end of the Self. No one wakes up through spiritual performance. The performance is the problem.

Awakening is not the grand finale of *your* story. It is the disappearance of the story entirely.
If that doesn't sound glamorous, it's because there's nothing left to enjoy it.

THE MYTH OF THE SEPARATE SELF
THE MOST EXPENSIVE LIE YOU EVER BOUGHT

Let's start with something you already believe without thinking about it: you are a person. A real, individual person. And you've been told this every day since you were born.

The training started before you could walk. Someone leaned over your crib and called you by a name. Someone took a picture and told you to smile. Someone said, "You're so smart," or "You're shy," or "You're a troublemaker." And just like that, the script began.

By the time you could talk, you could point to yourself and say "me." From then on, everything you saw and heard confirmed that you were this "me." You were praised for being a good version and scolded for being a bad one. You were fully assimilated into the reward-punishment paradigm. You learned to defend this 'me', improve it, punish it, shame it, adorn it, and educate it, all while striving to present it in the right light.

In other words, the "you" that you think you are was built, not born.

The idea of 'me' feels so obvious that questioning it seems silly. Of course, you're you. Who else would you be? You wake up in the same body every day. You answer to the same name. You remember the same life story. The evidence feels airtight.

Here's the first crack: Change any major input—*country, parents, language, culture*—and you'd be playing an entirely different "you." You'd look different, think differently, maybe even have a different personality. And in that other life, you'd feel just as certain that *that* version was the "real you."

So, which one is the real one? **The Truth:** Neither. What you call "yourself" is a bundle of memories, habits, and reactions tied together with a name tag. You didn't create it; it was issued to you. You're playing a role you didn't audition for, in a story you didn't write, surrounded by other actors convinced their roles are real too.

The separate Self survives by constant rehearsal. Every dinner plan, every memory replay, every imagined future conversation—it's all practice for the next scene. The moment rehearsal stops, even briefly, the act begins to wobble.

REMEMBER MIKE

Mike believed he was his own man. But if you looked closely, there was no "Mikeness" at all. His identity was stitched together from borrowed pieces. His sense of humor copied from friends. His taste in music lifted from the people he wanted to impress. His opinions recycled from whatever crowd he was standing in.

Every part of his character was propped up by the outside. When the room changed, Mike changed. When the group shifted, so did he. He called it personality, but it was just a collage of borrowed parts.

That's the myth of the separate self. What feels solid and unique is actually dependency disguised as individuality. The Ego insists on "me," but that "me" is nothing more than a patchwork of other voices, other gestures, other masks.

Even "spirituality" doesn't stop it. You hear, "The Self is an illusion," and nod, then get steps to make that illusion calmer, kinder, more loving.

You meditate to improve yourself. Forgive to improve yourself. "Let go" of Ego… to improve yourself. That's not dismantling the Self; it's sending it to a spa.

The separate Self isn't just *one* illusion among many. It is the projector. Every story about your life, purpose, struggles, and awakening depends on it running in the background. Stop the projector, and the whole movie disappears, no matter how gripping it was.

And yes, that scares most people. If the Self goes, what's left? Memories, relationships, goals—all of it changes in ways the Self can't survive. That might sound like loss, but it's actually the release of something that was never real in the first place.

Awakening isn't a glow you add to your self-image. It's what happens when belief in the Self stops, and when it stops, *you* are gone.

Not upgraded. Not healed. Gone.

And as you'll see later, this "you" is only one of five hidden supports keeping the whole simulation running. Pull them all, and nothing remains to prop up the show.

At The Bar:

You: "But if there's no me, who's going to read this book?"

Me: "Exactly. No one."

You: "That doesn't make sense. I'm sitting right here."

Me: "You're sitting in a story about someone who's sitting right here."

You: "So... I'm not real?"

Me: "You're real the way a dream character is real while you're dreaming. Convincing until you wake up. After that, it's just smoke."

You: "That's... unsettling."

Me: "It's only unsettling to the thing that doesn't survive. Everything else will be fine."

EGO ARCHITECTURE
MEET THE WARDEN OF YOUR INVISIBLE PRISON

Most people think of Ego as a personality trait: big Ego, small Ego, humble Ego, toxic Ego. Something that lives inside them, maybe in the head or the heart, and can be tuned up or toned down. That is the shallow end of the pool.

The reality is Ego is not a piece of you; it is the whole thing you think is you. It is not sitting in your mind like some internal parasite. It is the entire framework through which you see, think, feel, and experience reality. If Ego were gone, your entire world, not just your self-image, would disappear in the way you currently know it.

EGO: External Guided Observation

Think of Ego as "External Guided Observation." It is not a fixed inner object; it is a relational construct, an identity that forms by looking outward and referencing what it sees. The Ego says:

> "I am this because I see that."
> "I am good because I see what is bad."
> "I am successful because I measure against others."

It is a mirror, reflecting the external world back into a sense of self. No mirror, no "me."

Three behaviors keep this structure alive:

1. Reactive Construct: The Ego adapts to its surroundings like a chameleon, shifting its identity based on whatever is in front of it.

2. Boundary Setter: By defining "me" and "not me," it draws the lines of selfhood. Without an "out there" to contrast against, it has no way to know where it begins or ends.

3. Continuity Machine: By constantly updating itself with new external input, it keeps the story going without gaps.

A Quick Example:

Think about someone who acts differently depending on the room they are in. At work, they speak in professional jargon, drop buzzwords, and act confidently. With close friends, the same person cracks crude jokes, uses slang, and relaxes their body language. At a family dinner, they revert to old childhood habits, maybe even old speech patterns they don't use anywhere else.

That's the structure at work. The "Self" is not a fixed core; it's a shifting performance that takes its cues from whatever is around it. The identity changes because the reference points change. The mirror is always reflecting, but what it reflects, and the character it produces, depends entirely on the scene.

From this perspective, the Ego structure is the mirror, the reflective surface that makes identity possible. The Ego character is what appears inside that mirror. The character's movements, choices, and stories all happen within the structure, never outside it.

The structure and the character aren't the same thing, though they depend on each other like a stage depends on its lead actor, and the actor depends on the stage.

The Ego Structure is the hidden architecture. It's the rules, coding, and scaffolding that make "Self" possible at all. It sets the boundaries for what the Self can and can't be. It holds the belief in separation in place. It decides the size and shape of the stage, the lighting, and what counts as "on script" or "off script."

The Ego Character is the costume, voice, and personality you recognize as "me." It's the plotline, the emotional tone, the quirks, the fears, the ambitions. It's the visible part, the one other people interact with, but it's entirely shaped by the structure underneath.

A strong structure can make the character feel "internally solid," like they have a core no matter what happens around them. A weak or unstable structure will make the character need constant applause, validation, criticism, or reflection from others just to know they exist.

But here's the key: neither type is more real. The "self-sufficient" monk on a mountain and the "validation-hungry" influencer are running on the same operating system, the same structure, just with different resource needs.

Think of it like this: you could have a skyscraper built with steel beams that stand even in high winds, or a movie set façade that needs props and crew holding it up from behind. Both are still part of the same illusion. Remove the structure, and both vanish equally fast.

The Ego structure is the survival mechanism; the Ego character is the survival costume.

REMEMBER MIKE

Mike's uncle was the blueprint: ruthless, rich, untouchable. That model became his cage. He thought he was building success. He was just inhabiting a prefab prison. The invisible architecture dictated his choices: the cars, the drugs, the women, the business. He never questioned the walls because the walls looked like aspiration.

This is how Ego works: it hands you a blueprint and says *build your life here*. Mike did. And every brick reinforced the uncle's architecture. He never needed chains; he was already in the cell. Remember Mike: what you copy becomes what contains you.

The Whole Equation

$$EGO = \text{Ego Structure} + \text{Ego Character} = \textbf{Reality}$$

Ego Structure → the *invisible architecture* that makes any "Self" possible. It's the rules, boundaries, and survival wiring—the trellis.

Ego Character → the *visible performance* that plays out on that structure. It's the voice, style, and storyline—the vine.

The character is what you see and identify with, but it can't exist without the structure.

The structure can sit there without that specific character (and host another one later), but it's meaningless without a character to animate.

Together, they *are* the "you" and the "world" you think you live in.

Destroy one but not the other? The illusion rebuilds.

Keep both? The illusion runs forever.

Collapse both? That's the end, not just of the "you" inside reality, but of the reality inside "you."

Ego is Reality

This is where most people lose the thread. They think Ego is something that "shows up" inside a preexisting reality, person, or personality. They imagine they could "drop the Ego" and still have the same world, just with more peace and clarity. **That is not how it works.**

The world you experience is generated inside the Ego structure. The streets you walk, the people you meet, the thoughts you have about them—**all of it** appears inside the projection.

Which means your entire perception of **"reality" is Ego.** Not just the thoughts about yourself. Not just the emotions you like or dislike. The whole damn thing.

Remember the simulation we talked about earlier? This is it, not as some sci-fi fantasy where you are trapped in a giant computer, but as the living, breathing illusion you walk through every day.

The Ego structure is the code. The Ego character is the avatar. The "world" you see is just the rendered set where the story plays out.

Inside the simulation, everything looks real because it has to. Everything is generated inside this framework. And just like in a game, you never see the code running in the background; you only see the images it produces.

The trap is not that you are in the simulation. The trap is that you think it is reality. You think the set is the world. You think the actor is you.

How it Maintains Itself

Here's the tricky part: The Ego structure is self-healing. It feeds on continuity. Every memory you recall, every plan you make, every comparison you draw between yourself and the world is a fresh drop of fuel. It uses language to solidify itself. It uses time to stretch itself. It uses relationships to validate itself.

It even uses the idea of

"Destroying the Ego" or "Ego Death"

as a way to make itself more important.

The Ego character, the one you think is "you," is just the visible performance. The real survival mechanism is underneath, hidden in the structure itself.

You can change costumes all day long—rebel, saint, victim, hero—but if the theater is still standing, the show goes on.

True Awakening = Collapse of Both

This is where the awakening marketplace tricks you the most. They sell it like you get to keep the actor but ditch the stage, or that you get to keep the stage and just play a nicer, enlightened character.

Awakening is the collapse of the actor. The stage remains, but exposed as simulation-empty, unsupported, unreal. The actor is gone, and with it, the belief that the play was ever real.

The actor is gone. And there's nothing standing in its place.

🌀 **At The Bar:**

You: "So the Ego isn't just part of the story. It's the stage, the lights, the script, and the actor?"

Me: "Exactly. You've been living in a one-character play and calling it the universe."

You: "Wow… so if the Ego goes…"

Me: "…the play stops. The theater is gone. The stage crew quits. The popcorn machine catches fire. And you stop thinking you were ever in the building."

You: "So what's left then?"

Me: "Nothing you can picture. The playhouse doesn't get replaced with something else; it just isn't there anymore. There's no curtain drop, no encore. Just no theater. No actor. No audience. No performance at all."

You: "So… nothing?"

Me: "Not nothing like empty. Nothing like no pretend. The show's over, and without a show, there's no you to miss it."

SIMULATION EXPLAINED
THE CODE THAT WRITES "YOU" IN REAL TIME

Earlier we talked about the Ego structure being the stage, the lights, the sound, and the actor all rolled into one. That is the theater. Now we are going backstage to see the machinery that makes it run.

We are going to use the word "simulation." Don't drift into science fiction. This is not The Matrix. This is not a computer program in a secret lab. This is not aliens feeding you false images. The simulation is much closer than that. It is the entire reality you experience from the moment you wake up in the morning to the moment you fall asleep at night, and every dream you have in between.

Simulation is **structurally unreal**. That does not mean it does not appear. You see it, hear it, touch it, taste it, smell it. You have relationships inside it. You have pain and pleasure inside it. But it only holds together because the Ego structure is constantly rendering it. Pull the plug on the Ego, and the simulation collapses instantly.

If you doubt this, think about dreams. While you are dreaming, everything seems solid; the street you walk on, the voice of your friend, the weight of the coffee cup in your hand. But when you wake up, all of it disappears in a second. It did not fade. It did not dissolve. It stopped being rendered.

The same is true here, except this simulation runs on a more stable engine, with higher resolution and fewer glitches. That stability makes it convincing, not real. And if you start poking holes in it, the simulation has built-in ways to patch them before you even notice.

The "World Out There" Loophole

Right now, you might be thinking:

> *"Sure, my experience is personal and filtered, but trees, cars, and people are still "out there."*

Maybe. Maybe not. But here's the point: no one has ever, and can ever, experience "out there" directly.

Your eyes don't see objects. They detect patterns of light, electromagnetic waves bouncing off whatever's in front of you. Your brain takes those signals, processes them, and creates a picture. That picture is not the world. It is an internal rendering, a simulation inside the simulation.

This is not philosophy. This is basic neuroscience. Every single thing you see, hear, touch, taste, and smell is mediated by your nervous system. You never touch reality directly; you touch the model your brain creates of it.

The so-called "external world" is always experienced as an internal rendering.

And that's just the first layer of distance. On top of the raw sensory construction, there's another filter; the filter of your beliefs, conditioning, programming, and personal history.

The raw data is neutral. But the moment it is perceived, the character colors it:

> *Your upbringing tells you what is dangerous, safe, or desirable.*
> *Your cultural programming tells you what is beautiful, ugly, sacred, or profane.*
> *Your personal history tells you what to fear, chase, or avoid.*

By the time that neutral stream of data reaches "you," it has been fully shaped by layers of interpretation.

You are not experiencing reality; you are experiencing the world-as-processed-by-your-character.

⚡ REMEMBER MIKE

Rehab stripped Mike down, but the simulation rebuilt instantly. Tattoo. Designer watch. A "Rehab Survivor" persona. The code didn't pause; it simply re-rendered.

Ego doesn't need time. It reboots the moment the old Self falters.

Mike mistook his new skin for liberation. In truth, the program wrote another "Mike" in real time.

Simulation isn't content; it's the machinery generating identity. Mike was proof: even in breakdown, the system renders a new character.

Remember him when you imagine you've escaped. If a "you" appears, the simulation still runs.

The Simulation's Job

The simulation has one job:

Preserve the Self.

It does this in three ways:

1. Identity preservation: It keeps reflecting "you" back to yourself in every situation. Even when you are not thinking about yourself, you are at the center of the scene.

2. Continuity: It creates the illusion that there is one continuous thread of life unfolding for "you."

3. Narrative: It turns raw, meaningless appearances into "your story," with plot, progress, setbacks, and goals.

If any of these three functions stop, the Self cannot keep standing.

The Machinery

It relies on five moving parts to keep the rendering running:

1. Thought: Links moments together and tells you what they mean.

2. Time: Gives you "past" and "future," so the Self can imagine movement.

3. Image: Labels and fixes things as "known."

4. Contrast: Defines by opposites: good/bad, before/after.

5. Belief: Makes the whole construction feel unquestionable.

Take any one of these away, and the simulation stutters. Remove them all, and it stops rendering entirely.

The Five Pillars of Simulation

Think of the simulation as a house. It only stands because five load-bearing pillars hold it up. Take away one, and the structure begins to tilt. Knock out all five, and the house doesn't collapse slowly; it disappears instantly, like a dream dissolving the moment you wake up. Everything the simulation renders, every thought, sensation, memory, role, and even the sense of being "you" in a world—rests on five structural supports. Without them, nothing can stand.

Yes, **everything** in what we call **"reality"** (as rendered by the Ego) depends on the Five Pillars.

Here are the five:

1. Separation: *"I am here, everything else is out there."*

This is the voice of division. It makes a clean line between "me" and "you," "inside" and "outside." Without it, the idea of self vs. world cannot stand.

2. Continuity: *"I was, I am, I will be."*

This is the time-keeper. It tells you there is a thread running from past to present to future, all belonging to the same "me." Without it, identity has no spine.

3. Narrative: *"This happened because…"*

This is the storyteller. It turns random events into plotlines and interprets every appearance as part of "my journey." Without it, life stops feeling like a story at all.

4. Ownership: *"This is mine."*

This is the claim-staker. It attaches everything—thoughts, emotions, successes, failures—to a supposed center. Without it, experiences still appear, but they belong to no one.

5. Meaning: "This matters."

This is the evaluator. It stamps experiences as important, tragic, sacred, or purposeful. Without it, events still happen, but they carry no built-in significance.

To help you remember them, collapse them into an acronym:

SCNOM — Seeing Clearly Negates Obvious Manipulation.

Think of SCNOM like five mob bosses running the same racket.

- **Separation** collects the "me vs. you" tax.
- **Continuity** keeps charging rent for time you'll never actually live in.
- **Narrative** writes the headlines and makes sure you're always the main character.
- **Ownership** grabs every appearance and slaps a "mine" sticker on it.
- **Meaning** plays judge and jury, deciding what counts and what doesn't.

Individually, they look convincing. Together, they run the whole simulation. Every word you use, every memory you carry, every story you tell, pays rent to one of them.

(And yes, if you pick up the workbook, you'll meet SCNOM again. There, each pillar gets pulled apart by drills until the house can't stand.)

The Simulation Blueprint

Picture this as a three-layer machine.

Layer One: The Code

This is the Ego structure. It is invisible to you while you are inside it, just like you never see the source code of a computer game while you are playing.

The code determines how reality appears to you, not just what you see, but how you experience yourself as the one seeing it.

Layer Two: The Rendering

This is the simulation in action. The "world" appears. The "you" inside it appears. Thoughts, sensations, and events are stitched together into a moving picture.

It feels continuous because the code keeps refreshing the frames every instant.

Layer Three: The Functions

The simulation has three core purposes:

1. Keep "you" at the center of every scene.

2. Make it feel like there is a single life thread running from your past into your future.

3. Turn every appearance into part of "your story."

The Key Point

All of this—the code, the rendering, the functions, the machinery—is one system. The moment belief in the system fails, the rendering stops. The "world" and the "you" inside it collapse together. There is no "you" left to watch it happen.

"It's just my mind."

This is not solipsism. The simulation is not "your mind" imagining a world. The Ego structure is not a private daydream. It renders both the "world" and the "you" inside it together. They rise and fall as one.

"What about reprogramming?"

Some will think: *"If it's a simulation, I can just hack it. Change the code. Make a better dream."* That is still simulation. That is the character redecorating its own stage so it can keep performing. You don't "fix" the simulation. You either believe it and live inside it, or belief fails and it collapses.

"How do I get out?"

You don't. The character cannot walk off its own stage. Every step it takes is still part of the play. Collapse is not a choice or a technique. It happens when the supports fail under exposure.

Time is Not Passing

You have been trained from birth to believe time is moving forward like a river. It carries you from the past into the future. That is the picture you were given, and it feels true because the simulation is built to make it feel true.

But time is not an independent thing out there ticking away. It is a rendering tool, part of the machinery that keeps the simulation running.

Here's how it works.

The **"Past" is memory.** That's it. And memory is not a recording. It is not stored on a shelf somewhere in your brain like an old VHS tape you can rewind and watch again. Memory is a construction. Every time you "remember" something, you rebuild it in the present moment using the images, beliefs, and identity you currently hold. This means your so-called past changes to fit your current narrative. It is not evidence of anything. It is just another rendering, dressed up to look like history.

The **"Future" is projection**. It is the same machinery as memory, only flipped forward. You take pieces of what you think you know from the past and reassemble them into imagined possibilities. None of them exist. They are mental simulations running inside the larger simulation.

And then there's **"Now"**, the place you think is real. But in the simulation, "now" is not a timeless state of pure being.

It is just the current frame being rendered.

The next frame will replace it instantly. What you call "flowing time" is just your mind stitching those frames together, the way a movie projector turns still images into what looks like continuous motion.

If you have ever watched old film reels, you know each frame is separate. The movement you see is not actually there; it is an illusion created by the brain filling in the gaps. That is exactly how the simulation renders your life.

From within the simulation, it feels like you are moving forward in time, living your story. But structurally, nothing is moving. Only frames appearing, disappearing, and being linked into a sequence.

The one linking them all together is the Ego. Without time, there's no continuity. Without continuity, there's no Self.

The Simulation Strikes Back

Here's something you might not have considered yet:

The simulation is not alive, but it behaves like something protecting itself. Threaten its continuity, and it adapts instantly. The twist?

> **The "you" you think you are *is* that defense system.**

The Five Automatic Defense Moves

Whenever Collapse gets too close, here's how the simulation pulls you back in:

1. Refinement: The character gets a makeover.

You swap your old beliefs for "deeper," more "spiritual" ones.

> *"I understand non-duality now."*

Congratulations, the Ego just leveled up into a spiritual form. Same game, prettier graphics.

2. Deferral: Collapse gets moved to a safe distance.

> *"One day, I'll awaken."*

By turning Collapse into a future goal, the continuity of "me" stays perfectly intact.

3. Appropriation: Rupture moments get stolen and repackaged.

You have a destabilizing glimpse of the structure, and within days the Ego is telling the story:

> *"That was my awakening."*

The raw Rupture gets absorbed into the character's mythology—turning danger into a trophy.

4. Mystification: Collapse becomes mythical.

The simulation makes Collapse seem so rare, sacred, or cosmic that you can't possibly challenge it directly.

> *"Only saints in caves get this. Not me."*

It's untouchable, so you stop touching it.

5. Diversion: Brand-new problems arrive to "solve."

Suddenly there's a health scare, a new relationship, a financial crisis, or a "calling" you need to follow. Anything to keep the machinery busy, because a busy Self is a safe Self.

Why This Matters

These responses are not intentional. There's no evil mastermind pulling the strings. They're simply the natural functioning of the simulation, the same way a thermostat kicks on when the room cools. It is not *personal*.

Which means this:

- You will never dismantle "yourself" through "your own" effort, because the one doing the dismantling *is* the machinery.

- Every time you think you're "getting closer" through a new belief, insight, or method, check whether you've just upgraded the costume instead of removing it.

- Rupture moments are not enough on their own; without structural failure, the simulation can and will reabsorb them.

The simulation's defense system isn't a villain to be defeated. It's the game board itself. And until that board collapses, every move you make is still being played inside it.

When The Simulation Glitches

Every now and then, the seams show.

The rendering system that keeps "you" believing in a continuous world doesn't always run smoothly. Frames slip. Predictions land too cleanly. Memories misfire.

The Ego loves to dress these up as mystical: past lives, prophecies, cosmic signs. They're not proof of magic. They're proof of machinery.

Each so-called "mystical experience" is just the simulation hiccupping, the Five Pillars overlapping, stuttering, or mis-tagging in real time.

What follows are eight common examples of how the illusion flickers and the best explanations based on Simulation and the Structure.

They feel profound because the scaffolding bent for a second. But the fact that they can happen at all is the giveaway: reality isn't solid. It's stitched.

1) Déjà Vu

What people think it is:

A glitch in the Matrix. A memory from a past life. A sign you're "meant" to be where you are. Most explain it as remembering something that hasn't happened yet.

What's really happening:

Déjà Vu is a rendering glitch. The simulation stitches perception into seamless continuity. Normally, the tagging system marks "fresh perception" as present and "recalled perception" as past. But sometimes the tagging system misfires. The brain processes an incoming perception twice, once slightly out of sync. The second time it feels like memory because the first (microsecond earlier) processing already tagged it as "past."

Result: You feel like you've "been here before," but really the system just duplicated its own rendering.

Pillars active: Continuity (frames linked as timeline), Narrative (this happened already), Ownership (my memory), Meaning (this must matter).

2) Premonitions

What people think it is:

Prophecy. Intuition. Psychic ability. "I knew what was going to happen seconds before it did."

What's really happening:

The nervous system constantly simulates forward a few steps, predicting what will happen next so the character stays safe. Usually, it misses. Sometimes environmental cues + probability + timing make the prediction land perfectly. When it hits, the Narrative + Ownership pillars rewrite it as "I knew."

Result: A micro-prediction dressed up as supernatural foresight.

Pillars active: Continuity (projecting forward), Ownership (my foresight), Narrative (the prophecy story), Meaning (this was special).

3) Synchronicity

What people think it is:

"The universe sent me a sign." Coincidences interpreted as destiny, alignment, or cosmic choreography.

What's really happening:

In a closed-loop rendering where "you" and "world" co-arise, coincidences are mathematically inevitable. When they happen, the Meaning pillar slaps importance on them, and Narrative weaves them into your story arc. Ownership stamps it: "my synchronicity."

Result: Pure pattern overlap dressed as divine orchestration.

Pillars active: Meaning (this was for me), Narrative (part of my arc), Ownership (my sign), Continuity (I was led here), Separation (me vs. universe).

4) Out-of-body Experience / "watching myself"

What people think it is:

The soul leaving the body. A higher state of consciousness. Proof of spirit.

What's really happening:

Under stress, trauma, or novelty, the Ego shifts its stance from actor to witness. Instead of dissolving, Ownership relocates: "I am the one watching the one doing." It feels like floating above, but it's just a change in self-positioning.

Result: Still Ego, just the same act from a balcony seat.

Pillars active: Ownership (I am the observer), Separation (watcher vs. watched), Continuity (the observer thread never breaks), Meaning (this must be profound), Narrative (special mystical story).

5) Vivid Dreams

What people think it is:

Spiritual messages. Symbolic journeys. A truer reality than waking.

What's really happening:

Dreams and waking are both simulations. Dreams just run a looser ruleset with higher emotional tagging. When emotion is high, the rendering stamps the dream in bold font, so on recall it feels "more real than real." Nothing mystical, just amplified importance.

Result: A dream mistaken for revelation.

Pillars active: Narrative (night stories), Meaning (symbols to decode), Ownership (my dream), Continuity (my past showing up in sleep).

6) Time Slowing in Emergencies

What people think it is:

Reality bending. Entering a supernatural state of heightened awareness.

What's really happening:

Under acute stress, perception samples more "frames per second." Later recall plays those extra frames back as stretched duration. Time didn't slow; the tape just got denser.

Result: Survival rendering edits, not physics.

Pillars active: Continuity (elastic time-thread), Ownership (I survived in slow-mo), Narrative (the epic story of what happened), Meaning (the near-miss was a message).

7) Place Familiarity Without Memory

What people think it is:

Proof of past lives. Hidden memories. Energetic resonance.

What's really happening:

The recognition system compares new input to stored templates. Sometimes the match spikes without a real episode attached. The label "familiar" fires, but nothing backs it.

It's recognition math, not reincarnation.

Result: Pattern overlap misread as memory.

Pillars active: Narrative (I've been here before), Continuity (past bleeding into now), Ownership (my past), Meaning (this place is special to me).

8) Losing Time / "Flow"

What people think it is:

Alignment with purpose. Proof of being "in the zone." A mystical merger with activity.

What's really happening:

In absorption, the Ownership module goes quiet. Continuity isn't updated. When the stance returns, Narrative backfills the gap: "Where did the time go?" or "I was in flow." Nothing disappeared —just fewer self-checks written to memory.

Result: A bookkeeping gap, not transcendence.

Pillars active: Continuity (patched afterward), Ownership (I lost track), Narrative (I was in flow), Meaning (therefore it was valuable).

The Structural Point

None of these require mysticism. They're the Five Pillars doing their jobs, sometimes clumsily, sometimes theatrically. When something feels uncanny, run Lenswork:

- Which pillar stamped this as "for me"?
- What happens if Meaning or Ownership is removed?
- Without Continuity/Narrative, is anything special left, or just appearance?

What Ends it?

The simulation can't end itself. Every move the Self makes to end it just becomes more simulation. Collapse happens only when belief in the system fails without repair. When that happens, both the "world" and the "you" collapse together.

And here's the Final Cut:

Collapse isn't escape from the simulation. It's the deletion of the one who could ever be trapped in the first place.

At The Bar:

You: "So you're saying none of this is real?"

Me: "It's real inside the simulation. Just not structurally real."

You: "What's the difference?"

Me: "The same difference between a dream and the bed you wake up in. One vanishes when the projection stops. The other is what remains."

(A long pause. The bar TV flickers above the counter. You glance up. Bright lights, applause, music. The bartender fades. The bar stools vanish. Suddenly, you're not in the bar anymore—you're in a studio.)

[Cue Jeopardy theme song]

Alex Trebek's voice:

"Welcome to another round of *Jeopardy!* Tonight's contestants are: Maria, a devoted Christian from Detroit; Stuart, a veteran Non-Dualist from San Francisco; Dr. Richards, a physicist from Boston; and last but not least, Philip, a Lensworker from Jacksonville."

[Audience applause]

Alex: "Tonight's categories are… Separation, Continuity, Narrative, Ownership, and, our final category, Meaning!"

(The audience claps. Spotlights sweep across the stage.)

Alex: "Maria, you've been chosen to start."

Maria: "Thank you, Alex. I'll take *Ownership* for $200."

Alex: "The answer is: *This invisible force convinces you something belongs to you, even when nothing does.*"

Maria: "What is God?"

[Buzzer sound]

Alex: "Sorry, that is incorrect. Stuart?"

Stuart: "What is awareness?"

[Buzzer sound]

Alex: "Sorry, also incorrect. Philip?"

Philip: "What is simulation?"

Alex: "Yes, correct." *(Applause)*

"Simulation holds up Ownership. Without it, there's no 'mine.' Philip, the board is yours."

Philip: "I'll take *Continuity* for $300."

Alex: "The answer is: *This creates the sense of a single life-thread stretching from birth to death.*"

Dr. Richards: "What is time?"

[Buzzer sound]

Alex: "Close, but not quite. Maria?"

Maria: "What is the soul?"

[Buzzer sound]

Alex: "Incorrect. Philip?"

Philip: "What is simulation?"

Alex: "Correct again!" *(Audience cheers.)*

[Maria frowns, Stuart looks annoyed]

Alex: "Next category?"

Philip: "Separation for $400."

Alex: "The answer is: *This trick makes 'you' appear here, and 'everything else' appear out there.*"

(Stuart slams his buzzer.)

Stuart: "What is Duality?"

Alex: "Sorry, incorrect. Dr. Richards?"

Dr. Richards: "What is the brain?"

[Buzzer sound]

Alex: "Sorry, Philip?"

Philip: (calmly) "What is simulation?"

Alex: "Correct again. Simulation renders separation."

(The game keeps rolling. Category after category. Every contestant struggles, but every correct response is the same. Philip sweeps the board.)

Alex (final round):

"And now for Final Jeopardy. The category is… Meaning. The clue is: *This convinces you that what happens in the dream matters to the dreamer.*"

(The Jeopardy theme plays. Maria writes "God." Stuart writes "Awareness." Dr. Richards writes "Entropy." Philip writes… "Simulation.")

Alex: "The correct response is… simulation. Congratulations, Philip, you are tonight's winner. In fact… you were the only player who ever had a chance."

Alex: "And remember, folks: in this game, there's only ever one answer. Simulation. Goodnight."

(The applause echoes, but the lights begin to dim. The stage collapses into static. You're back at the bar. Your drink is still in your hand. The bartender is polishing a glass like nothing happened.)

Me: "See? No matter the category, no matter the question, the answer never changes."

THE TRAP OF LANGUAGE
HOW WORDS BUILD THE CAGE YOU LIVE IN

Language is the Ego's most trusted weapon. Not money. Not fame. Not power. Words.

Language doesn't just describe reality; it builds it. It gives the Ego structure its walls and the Ego character its costume. It gives names to things so they seem solid, separates "me" from "you," "inside" from "outside," "good" from "bad."

Without language, the Ego can't narrate. Without narration, there is no story. Without story, there is no Self.

The Invisible Glue

When you say *"I,"* you glue the entire world back together with yourself in the center.

When you say *"my job," "my past," "my feelings,"* you reattach the character to its stage.

When you call something *"beautiful," "ugly," "wrong,"* or *"right,"* you fix it into the character's worldview.

Language doesn't just communicate ideas; it pins them down so they cannot dissolve.

And every single time, those words are secretly funding the Five Pillars, what we now call **SCNOM**:

- **Separation** ("I am here, you are there")
- **Continuity** ("I was, I am, I will be")
- **Narrative** ("This happened because…")
- **Ownership** ("This is mine")
- **Meaning** ("This matters")

SCNOM = Seeing Clearly Negates Obvious Manipulation.

Remember this acronym. Every word you speak props up one or more of these pillars.

But I'm Just Talking, Right?

That's the trap. You think words are harmless. Just labels. Just conversation.

But every pronoun you use—I, me, mine ze, hir, xem, xirs—whatever might be hip right now or is the pronoun flavor of the month, it reloads the Ego's operating system.

Every description you give keeps the story alive. And you do this automatically, without thinking, dozens or hundreds of times a day. Even when you "try" to use language carefully, the Ego finds a way to use that effort to make itself more real.

Example:

Someone says:

> "I'm trying to be more mindful of not saying 'I' so much."

Great intention, but notice what happens.

Now the Ego becomes *the one who is mindful of language.*

The identity just got a makeover.

Same structure. New outfit.

If you tag it **SCNOM-style**, you can see the whole trap:

- **Ownership:** *"I"* am the one doing it.
- **Continuity:** I have "been" careless before, but now I'm "mindful."
- **Narrative:** This is "my practice."
- **Meaning:** It matters that I'm careful.
- **Separation:** Me vs. those who are sloppy with words.

All five pillars, all in one "mindful" sentence.

Why Spiritual Language Is the Worst

In regular conversation, Ego keeps the character alive with casual talk. In "spiritual" conversation, Ego upgrades its costume.

- "I" becomes "this body" or "the Self."
- The character becomes "awakened," "aligned," or "present."
- It learns to say "there is no Self" while enjoying the role of *the enlightened one who can say that.*

Ego loves spiritual vocabulary because it makes the structure invisible while making the character look profound.

The Ego's Double Trick

First, it uses language to convince you the world is real and that you are in it.

Then, it uses more language to convince you that you are "seeing through" the illusion while keeping the talker firmly in place.

This is why you can't "talk" your way to Collapse. The talking *is* the continuity.

Everyday Proof

Watch what happens if you try to go an entire day without saying "I" or "me."

At first, it feels awkward. Then you start finding clever ways to get around it:

> Instead of *"I need coffee,"* you say, *"Coffee is needed."*
> Instead of *"I like that,"* you say, *"There is enjoyment."*

Congrats, you've just made the Ego a grammar expert.

Language Creates Separation

Even if you dropped every "I" and "me," the Ego still hides in the rest of your vocabulary.

Why? Because **words also slice reality into parts.**

- *Here* and *there* suggests distance.
- *This* and *that* suggest boundaries.
- *Self* and *other* suggests division.

You may think you are describing reality, but you are actually carving it into pieces, giving each piece a name, and pretending those pieces exist independently.

The moment you say "tree," you have separated that shape from the air around it. The moment you say "sky," you have drawn a line where there is none.

This is the first function of language: to cut the seamless appearance into digestible chunks so the **Ego can have a position in relation to them.** Without those cuts, the "me" has nowhere to stand.

Language as Memory Storage

The Ego doesn't just use language to describe the past; it uses it to *store* the past.

"My childhood" is not your childhood. It's a label, a bookmark, a compressed file. Behind it sits a vault of mental images, feelings, and stories that the Ego can call up at will.

Without language, those memories would fade quickly, like footprints in sand. But the Ego keeps repeating the words, which refresh the memory each time. Every re-telling, even in your own head, strengthens the illusion that it all happened exactly as described.

This is why a Self feels so solid: you are walking around with a constantly updated verbal archive of "your" life.

Language as Authority

Language doesn't just come from you. Much of it comes from outside: parents, teachers, books, culture, religion, politics.

Some phrases get repeated so often that they stop being questioned.

"Life is hard."
"You have to be someone."
"Good things happen to good people."

These phrases are like background code running in the operating system. Every time you use them, you reinforce the authority they carry. You may think you are just talking, but you are actually signing a contract with a worldview that was handed to you.

This is one reason the Ego clings to group language. It feels safe inside a shared code, where everyone agrees on the same definitions. It means the structure will not be challenged.

Interruption

Keep reading, and you will try to "use" this insight.

You will speak more carefully, swap "I" for clever grammar, and congratulate yourself for "seeing."

That is still selfing.

The trap is not in the words. It's in the one who claims to be avoiding them.

Language Creates Time

Time feels real because language keeps stitching it together. Without words, **"past"** and **"future"** don't exist. There's **only what's appearing.**

But language lets you:

> Name yesterday.
> *("I was this, now I'm that.")*

> Describe tomorrow.
> *("I will be this later.")*

> Link unrelated frames into one continuous life.
> *("I went there, now I'm here.")*

This is how language renders continuity, the lifeline of the Self.

⚡ REMEMBER MIKE ⚡

In group sessions, Mike became "the wise one." Not because he had clarity, but because he had mastered the words. He listened carefully, then repeated back the language of those further along. He quoted, he echoed, he rearranged phrases until they sounded like his own.

Each time he spoke, heads nodded. He was admired, respected.

But this was not wisdom. This was the trap of language. Words became the currency of his new identity. He didn't dissolve; he performed. Every borrowed phrase patched the cracks in his trellis. Every clever sentence reinforced the cage.

The performance of wisdom replaced the possibility of demolition.

Mike's story shows how words can seduce. The more he talked, the more he believed his own story. He mistook fluency for freedom. In truth, his mouth was busy constructing new bars. He could silence his body's craving with clever speech, but the machinery underneath kept running.

Language never saved him. It only bought him credibility while keeping him chained. His "wisdom" was simply another costume. Remember Mike when you feel tempted to narrate your own liberation. Words point, but they do not cut.

🔖 At The Bar:

You: "So you're telling me language is the whole problem?"

Me: "Not the whole problem, but it's the duct tape holding the whole mess together."

You: "So if I just stop saying 'I'…"

Me: "Then you'll be the smug guy at the bar who never says 'I.' Congratulations, you're now the enlightened weirdo who still has an Ego; it just speaks in bad poetry."

You: "So which words are safe to use?"

Me: "None. Every word pays rent to one of the Five Pillars. And the landlord never misses a payment."

You: "So silence is the answer?"

Me: "Silence still gets narrated as silence. The Ego's voiceover doesn't quit just because you stop talking."

You: "So what's left?"

Me: "Notice. Noticing doesn't save you. But it starves the code of your belief. That's the only crack in the system."

THE BODY-MIND HOAX
THE FAKE DIVORCE THAT KEEPS YOU CHASING

From the time you could speak, you were taught to split yourself in two.

"My body" over here.
"My mind" over there.

And somewhere above or behind them, "me," the one who supposedly owns both.

The school nurse told you to "listen to your body."

Your teacher told you to "use your mind."

Your religion told you the body is a temporary shell and the soul is forever.

Your doctor works on your body; your therapist works on your mind. Everywhere you turn, the split is reinforced.

Two things in relationship. Two systems that can be "balanced" or "aligned."

And you, the owner, supposedly in charge of managing the harmony.

It's one of the most convincing illusions the Ego ever built. Why?

Because as long as you believe body and mind are separate, you will spend your whole life trying to fix, upgrade, or negotiate between them, without ever noticing that the "you" in the middle is the real hoax.

How the Split Is Made

In reality, there's no line where "body" ends and "mind" begins.

The split exists only in language:

> "I have a body." (Owner + object)
> "I think." (Owner + action)

The moment you say those words, you've invented a middleman, the "me" who supposedly has a body and does thinking. That's the Ego's foothold. From there, it plays both sides.

> "I am my mind, trapped in this body."
> "I am my body, but my mind is ruining my peace."

Even if you merge them into "body–mind," Ego will sneak in as "the one watching the body–mind."

That watcher is not outside the loop; it is the loop in disguise.

How Culture and Spirituality Keep It Alive

Science historically treated the body like a machine and the mind like software running inside it.

Religion often flipped it; the mind or soul is eternal, the body is disposable. Spirituality upgraded the same split, swapping in language like:

"You are not the body. You are the eternal awareness in which the body appears."

Sounds profound, right? It's still the split, just dressed in non-dual robes.

Only now "you" identify with the awareness side, gazing at a "body" over there.

Ego doesn't care if you identify with flesh or light, as long as you identify with something.

The One-System Reality (Why There Aren't Two)

What you call "mind" and what you call "body" are just different camera angles on the same loop.

Change the angle; you change the language. Not the reality.

- **Thought appears** → breath shifts → heart rate changes → muscles engage → hormones release → posture adjusts → perception narrows.

This whole loop lands as "me, feeling this way about that."

- **Flip it:** a sound startles → diaphragm freezes → chemistry spikes → thought appears to explain the feeling.

Same loop, different entry point.

Key point: There is no thought that doesn't have a bodily echo, and there is no bodily state that doesn't invite a story.

One system. One simulation. One field of awareness modulating itself.

This doesn't mean every stubbed toe or virus has a hidden childhood origin. But whatever happens, accident, illness, or windfall, still runs through the same one-system filter.

The body and mind will both adapt to fit the story you already live in.

Addiction: The Loop That Feeds Itself

If you want a front-row seat to how the body–mind hoax really works, look at addiction.

It's one of the purest examples of a one-system loop running without a separate "you" driving it.

Addiction is not proof of your weakness, your brokenness, or your moral failure. It's just proof that a loop, once established, tends to keep feeding itself, with or without your permission.

Here's how it plays out:

1. Sensation leads the way.

A craving starts in the body, a tightness in the chest, a restless buzzing in the muscles, a low throb in the gut.

The system registers it as "something missing" or "something wrong."

2. The story jumps in.

A thought appears to explain the sensation:

> "I need a drink."
> "I need to check my phone."
> "I need just one more episode."

The craving gets a name and a target.

3. Action happens.

> The drink is poured.
> The app is opened.
> The episode plays.

For a moment, the craving sensation shifts, and the system registers that shift as "success."

4. Loop reinforced.

The body logs the chemical change as a win. The mind logs the story:

> "When I feel this way, doing this fixes it."

Next time the same sensation appears, the loop fires faster.

> **No "you" had to choose any of that.**

It's the same one-system reality, sensation and thought feeding each other until the next round.

The Overcoming Trap

In the simulation, "overcoming" addiction usually means swapping one loop for another.

The old pattern gets replaced with a new identity:

> "I'm sober."
> "I'm in recovery."
> "I'm the disciplined one now."

Nothing wrong with being sober or recovering, but if the Self is still at the center claiming it, the machinery hasn't stopped. It's just wearing a cleaner outfit.

This is why so many people "quit" one thing only to find themselves hooked on something else:

The system wasn't just after the drink, the hit, or the scroll.

It was after the stabilizing sensation that came from being someone in relation to the craving.

Addiction Rebrands

Even when you see this, the Ego will try to sneak back in:

The Spiritual Addict: trading the old habit for endless retreats, meditations, or energy healings.

The Health Purist: replacing the craving with hyper-control over food, supplements, or workouts.

The Recovery Guru: turning your story into a platform to "help others," while secretly feeding on the role.

Same loop. Different costume.

Addiction, seen this way, is just one more proof of the body–mind hoax:

> **No** split between thought and sensation.
> **No** separate "you" making it happen.
> Just **one** system, looping until it doesn't.

⚡ REMEMBER MIKE ⚡

Mike excused relapse by splitting himself in two: "My body is hooked, but my mind is strong." The hoax is this fake divorce. It keeps you chasing between halves that do not exist.

He believed his mind could *will* his body into obedience. He believed his body's failings left his mind untouched. Both were lies. The craving and the rationalization were one system.

The split let him keep drinking while believing he was winning.

Remember Mike when you feel tempted to separate body and mind.

The split is the hoax. The chase is the cage.

The Pipeline: From Belief to Biology (and Back)

> Belief → Perception → State → Physiology → Behavior → Environment → Reinforcement.

It always begins with a belief. Not the kind you debate in philosophy class, the kind you live in without knowing it.

Something like:

> "I am not safe."
> "I'm unworthy."
> "I'm alone."

This belief is not a sentence in your head. It's a lens over your perception.

With it on, your attention scans for proof. You notice the dangerous things, the dismissive looks, the empty chair in the corner, and ignore what doesn't match.

Your emotional climate adjusts to match the forecast:

Anxiety becomes the weather. Or sadness. Or anger.

Your physiology then changes to fit the new climate:

The nervous system leans toward "brace mode." Hormones tilt toward stress chemistry. The immune system adjusts for survival over long-term health.

Behavior follows:

You avoid. You overwork. You please. You explode.

Your environment rearranges to match the pattern.

You end up in relationships, jobs, and routines that reinforce the belief. And then the loop closes.

You point at your life and say:

"See? This is just who I am."

At that point, the belief isn't just in your head; it's in your shoulders, your gut, your sleep patterns, your blood chemistry.

Your state has become your trait. Your settings have become your Self. And your body has become the archive that proves the story true.

The Body as the Character's Archive

Your body is not just the vehicle carrying the story of "you."

It's the storage medium.

Posture is a paragraph.
Shoulders forward? Head down? That's a chapter on vigilance and submission. Chest open, jaw set? That's a chapter on dominance or defense.

Breath pattern is punctuation.
The pause before an exhale. The rush to inhale. The shallow, quick rhythm of an argument that never ended.

Muscle tone is the font.
Tense and sharp, or soft and collapsed, the tone tells you whether the story is "I fight" or "I give up."

Fascia is the binding.
This connective tissue wraps it all, stiffening around the story like a book cover that's been bent and hardened over years.

Chemistry is the ink.
Cortisol, adrenaline, serotonin, histamine, the biochemical language that keeps rewriting the same plotline every day.

When a pattern repeats, the system makes it cheaper to run. That cheaper setting becomes the "new normal."

That "new normal" becomes how you sit, stand, speak, digest, and sleep. And eventually, how you get sick.

This isn't mystical. It's mechanical.

If the system receives the instruction "brace" often enough, it will brace even when nothing's happening. The brace is not holding the memory.

It is the memory.

How Story Becomes Sensation

Here's what it looks like in real time:

You're at a dinner with friends. Someone says something that, without you realizing, resembles the tone your father used when he dismissed you as a kid.

Your system **predicts danger** based on that resemblance.

Preparation happens instantly:

> Muscles tense. Breath shortens. Blood rushes to your limbs. Adrenaline and cortisol flood your bloodstream.

Then a thought rises to explain the sudden readiness:

> "I can't handle this conversation."

That thought makes sense to you; after all, the body feels like it's in danger.

But here's the issue:

Repeat this enough times, and the body runs the sequence without the original thought. The sensation itself becomes "proof" of the story:

> Tight chest? That must mean panic.
> Knotted stomach? That must mean "I'm not safe."

You call it anxiety. The system calls it readiness.

The Ego calls it proof that "I" exist.

Pain as Proof

Pain is one of the Ego's slickest survival tools. Why?

Because sensation is convincing.

The moment pain spikes, the "me" feels solid. It feels undeniable.

> A heavy back keeps the "I carry everything" story alive.
> A tight throat keeps "I can't speak" believable.
> A clenched jaw keeps "I must hold it together" running.
> A rigid pelvic floor keeps "I'm not safe here" always on standby.

None of this is "in your head." It's in your one system.

And as long as the system needs the identity, it will keep the sensations that justify it.

Trauma as Configuration

Trauma is not just a memory you occasionally bump into. It's a *configuration*, a set of survival responses that got stuck halfway through and never shut off.

Fight energy with nowhere to go becomes migraines, jaw clench, shoulder armor.

Flight energy stuck at the door becomes restless legs, shallow breathing, gut churn.

Freeze becomes dissociation, numbness, chronic fatigue.

Fawn (appease) becomes over-smiling, a soft voice, a collapsed chest.

The body "remembers" because it's still trying to finish the action it wasn't allowed to complete. It's not punishing you. It's trying, eternally, to protect you the only way it knows how.

Why the Body Stores the Story

The body's not stupid. It's not storing tension and pain for fun. It's doing it for three main reasons:

1. Survival Efficiency:

If something "worked" once (even if it was awful), the system automates it. You survived; that's enough for the body to make it a default.

2. Social Belonging:

Many of your tensions are actually loyalty contracts to family culture:

"We don't cry."

"We never rest."
"We stay small."

3. Identity Maintenance:

Sensation stabilizes the narrative. If the body stopped broadcasting its proof, the "me" would feel optional. The Ego can't risk that.

Important: Believing your body is more sensitive, more blocked, or more traumatized than others is just the Ego running the "specialness" program through flesh.

It's the same ownership reflex, just wearing a diagnostic label.

The Ego will also flip the script into hopelessness: "I'm too damaged to ever change."

This is just specialness in a different costume; instead of being the most awakened or the most sensitive, you're now the most broken.

Either way, the identity stays central, and the body keeps proving it true.

Why Conventional Fixes Often Fail (Even When They Help)

Most people try to handle this body–mind conspiracy the same way they handle everything else in the simulation:

Find a tool. Apply the tool. Hope the problem disappears.

And sometimes, yes, it works for a while.

But structurally? The reason it doesn't stick is that the **archivist is still on the payroll.**

The identity, the one who needs the symptom, is still running the show.

Let's break down the most common "fix" strategies:

Cognitive-only work:

You talk about the pattern. You journal it. You "understand" it.

But the body is still running the loop. The shoulders still brace when the phone rings. The gut still flips when you see that name. Understanding is like describing the lock; it doesn't open it.

Somatic-only catharsis:

You cry, shake, scream into a pillow. You feel amazing for three days. Then you notice the same tension creeping back in. Why? Because the Ego just rebranded itself as "the one healing."

The loop remains; it's just wearing new gym clothes.

Biohacks and gadgets:

You take supplements, track sleep, use red light therapy.

Chemistry shifts for a bit, but your sovereignty is now outsourced to a device. When the gadget's gone, so is your "regulation."

Spiritual bypass:

You tell yourself "There is no Self, so there's no problem."

Meanwhile, your jaw is welded shut and your breath is shallow. That's not freedom; that's cosplay. Helpful? Sure. Final? No.

Because as long as the archivist keeps their job, the archive refills.

One more trap worth catching: the "future fantasy" of the perfectly regulated body.

If your vision of health still has "me" as the central character living in it, you've just moved the finish line instead of dropping the race.

The Clean Way Out

You don't "fix" a one-system reality by fighting it.

You don't need to dismantle the body or the mind. You simply stop feeding the parts that keep misfiring.

There are three moves, simple, repeatable, and ruthless:

1) See: Name What's Happening, Not Who You Are.

> Drop possessives. Drop the "my."
> Instead of "my anxiety," try "tightness in chest is present."
> Instead of "I'm overwhelmed," try "thoughts of overwhelm are here."

Grammar detox loosens the identity that owns the state.

2) Suspend: Interrupt Ownership for 10–30 seconds. Ask:

> Did I choose this thought to appear?
> Does this sensation announce an owner?
> Does awareness have edges?

Don't try to "answer," just rest in the pause that follows. The doer can't fit through that doorway.

3) Stand: As What Remains.

For 60–180 seconds, let the experience self-arrive without a center managing it.

If a "watcher" shows up, label it as a watcher-thought and return to just what's here.

Do this dozens of times a day in small windows.

Tiny, consistent cuts beat one "heroic" breakthrough every time.

Somatic De-Identification: Knobs You Can Actually Turn

These are not magic spells. They're practical levers you can use to unhook the story from the sensation:

- **Breath:** Let exhales be longer than inhales for 2 minutes. Don't do relaxation; allow it.

- **Eyes:** Include peripheral vision. Narrow gaze narrows the sense of "me."

- **Jaw & Tongue:** Unclench. Let the tongue rest heavy. The mind follows the tongue.

- **Hands & Feet:** Press palms together and release. Feel your soles. Ownership drops when contact rises.

- **Orienting:** Slowly scan the room, naming five safe objects. Show the animal you're not back "there."

- **Completion:** If you feel the urge to push/run/voice, let 2% of it express safely into a pillow or wall.

- **Pendulation:** Touch the easiest spot in your body, then the hardest, back and forth. Teach contrast.

- **Ethical Congruence:** Tell the plain truth in small doses. Nothing dysregulates the body like living a lie.

Guardrail:

Don't chase big releases. Chasing is the Ego in gym shorts.

The Part You Were Hoping We Wouldn't Say

You can stretch, massage, and meditate for years and keep the Self that needs the tension.

You can become exquisitely regulated and exquisitely identified.

You can become the calmest person in the room, and still be the character maintaining that calm as an identity.

The body stops shouting when no one needs the noise to feel real.

That's the end of the conspiracy:

> **Not** mind over body.
> **Not** body over mind.
> **But the quiet fall of the owner.**

Yes, you can break a bone and it has nothing to do with a childhood story, but your recovery, your pain, and even your relationship to the injury will still run through the same one-system filter.

When that happens, nothing "heals."

> There's just less to maintain.
> Less to defend. Less to prove.

And in the space that's left, the system finally does what it always wanted to do:

It relaxes into the ordinary, unbranded grace of being alive.

> **No** halos. **No** hashtags. **No** hero.
> **Just this.**

At The Bar:

You: "So... are you saying my illness is my fault?"

Me: "No. Fault is a morality game. We're talking mechanics, not morality. Lots of variables—genes, environment, accidents, viruses—come into play. Identity patterns just happen to be one variable you can actually influence. Compassion wins. Blame doesn't."

You: "But what about genetics? My family's full of bad backs and bad tempers."

Me: "Genes load the gun. Experience pulls the trigger. Change the experience—felt safety, honesty, rest, belonging—and the gene expression changes. It's not magic; it's wiring."

You: "So I can just think myself healthy?"

Me: "Nope. Positive thinking is like spraying perfume on a dumpster. Smells better for five minutes; trash is still rotting underneath. What works is stripping the identification and creating real safety. Then the system fixes what it can."

You: "Should I stop seeing doctors?"

Me: "Only if you want to roleplay as a cautionary tale. Use medicine, surgery, therapy when needed. Treat the body and unplug the story fueling the pattern. It's both/and, not either/or."

You: "Why did my symptoms get worse when I started this?"

Me: "Because frozen systems thaw noisy. That's not failure; that's progress. Go slower. Smaller doses. More truth, fewer heroics."

You: "How long is this going to take?"

Me: "There's no cosmic stopwatch. Signs you're on track: less compulsion, faster recovery after triggers, simpler preferences, more ordinary joy, fewer stories about yourself."

You: "The pain moved. Did I just invent a new problem?"

Me: "Or your system is reorganizing. Symptoms often migrate when underlying patterns start to unwind. Follow the function, not the whack-a-mole game of sensation."

You: "Do I need some big, sobbing, screaming catharsis to heal?"

Me: "Not unless you're auditioning for a movie. Sometimes it happens; sometimes it doesn't. The only thing that matters is less identification, not bigger fireworks."

You: "Can I still use medication?"

Me: "Absolutely. Stabilizers can give you the platform to loosen identity. This isn't a purity contest."

You: "What if my trauma is really bad?"

Me: "Then you bring in skilled support. You prioritize. Safety first, safety second, safety third. This is not a bravery competition."

You: "So the Ego's okay with me healing?"

Me: "Oh, it loves it. The Ego will happily let you heal forever, as long as it gets to be the one doing the healing."

SELF-HELP TRAP
WHEN THE SOLUTION IS JUST A BETTER-BRANDED PROBLEM

Picture this. You're wandering through a massive marketplace, stalls everywhere, bright banners flapping in the breeze.

One vendor is selling

> **"Confidence in 30 Days."**

Another is offering

> **"The 5 Steps to Your True Purpose."**

And, a charismatic guy with perfect teeth is promising

> **"Limitless You."**

It all smells amazing, hope mixed with cinnamon buns.

You're not here for cinnamon, though. You're here because you've been told something's wrong with you. Not wrong like need-a-doctor wrong, but wrong like **you-could-be-so-much-more** wrong.

So, you try one. Then another. And another. And each time, you get that little buzz of possibility:

> "Yes… this time I'm going to get there."

What you don't notice is the person running the market owns every stall. They sold you the "problem" pamphlet at the front gate. They're renting you the ladder you're climbing. They even designed the badge you get to wear when you "level up."

And here's the problem: that market owner? **It's you.**

Or rather, it's the **character** you've been calling **"me."**

And before we go further, let's settle a question your Ego is already whispering:

> "But isn't self-help good if it makes life better?"

Sure, if what you're after is a smoother ride inside the same cage. This isn't about whether self-help makes you feel better for a while; it often does. It's about the one thing it will never do: dismantle the "you" it's built to serve.

The Ego's Best Magic Trick

It's not just that the Ego plays both sides of the game; it is the game. It creates the sense of a broken "me" who needs fixing, then sells itself the role of fixer, healer, seeker, achiever. From the moment you pick up that first self-help book, the rules are already set:

> **You start broken.**
> **You end "better."**
> **And in between, you get to be the hero of your own story.**

It feels noble. It feels exciting. It feels like the right thing to do. And that's why you rarely notice the cost: you've agreed to keep the one thing alive that is never questioned, the **"you"** at the center.

And if you think this chapter is going to tell you how to "do self-help better"…

Sorry. That stall is closed. We're here to burn the whole marketplace down.

Loop in Plain Sight

Most people think self-help is a ladder. You climb enough rungs, you'll reach freedom.

But when you step back, it's a treadmill, always moving, never arriving. Here's how it plays out in real life:

1. Feel Broken: The starting gun is always a sense of lack. Sometimes it's loud ("I'm a mess"), sometimes quiet ("I could be better"). Either way, the Ego plants the seed.

2. Claim Ownership: The unease gets branded as my problem, my flaw, my trauma.

3. Seek Solutions: You go hunting. Courses, coaches, books, retreats, podcasts. Every one promises to take you from where you are to where you want to be.

4. Feel a High: That first hit of "I'm making progress" is intoxicating. The identity feels alive, relevant, and on a journey.

5. Adjust the Target: The high fades, and the Ego shifts the goalpost:

> "I just need a better method, deeper work, more time."

6. Repeat Forever: Welcome back to step one.

From inside the loop, it feels like growth. From outside, it's a hamster wheel in designer packaging.

Why It Works So Well

The self-help loop works because it never threatens its own foundation.

It runs on one unquestioned assumption:

> **"There is a real you here who can be improved."**

Every method, every habit tracker, every breakthrough session operates from this premise. And why wouldn't it? If that premise falls apart, the entire industry, and the entire Ego structure, has nothing to sell and nowhere to go.

This is why the loop can last for decades.

It's not a conspiracy; it's a design feature. The system is built to preserve the "you," no matter how much you change the paint color on the walls.

New Uniform, Same Prison

Imagine a prison guard walking into your cell, tossing you a brand-new uniform, and saying:

> "You're free now. Look, it's a better color!"

The room hasn't changed. The walls are exactly where they were. But your brain registers "something new" and calls it progress.

That's self-help: it changes the feel of the prison, not the fact of it.

Your identity gets a facelift, but the structure, the idea of "me," stays untouched.

Ego-Trap Warnings

Even seeing the scam doesn't automatically set you free.

The Ego is slippery, and it will rebrand itself instantly if it sees an opening.

Here's how the trap replays itself after you've spotted it:

The "I'm Above Self-Help" Badge: You now identify as the one who "gets it" and look down on those who don't.

The Anti-Self-Help Persona: You build a new identity around rejecting self-help, making that your new badge of specialness.

The Awakened Consumer: You still buy courses and books, convincing yourself they're "different" because you see through the old kind.

The Savior Role: You start "freeing" others from the loop so you can be the enlightened rescuer.

The Loop Awareness Trap: You congratulate yourself for "seeing the loop" while quietly building a subtler one you can feel superior about escaping.

Notice the theme? In every case, the "me" is still alive; only the costume has changed.

Not Just Self-Help

Self-help is only one of the arenas where this loop plays out.

The Ego is an opportunist, and any domain that offers identity, validation, or a sense of control is fair game.

Let's walk through some of the other popular stages where the same drama plays out:

Spiritual Seeking: Chasing awakening, enlightenment, or blissful states while strengthening the seeker identity.

Relationships & Love: Looking for "the one" or reshaping yourself to become lovable, always anchoring your worth to someone else's approval.

Career & Success: Defining your value by promotions, titles, and accomplishments, never noticing the bar keeps moving.

Health & Fitness: Using diet, exercise, or wellness to "perfect" the body and lock in a controlled self-image.

Politics & Ideology: Making morality or belief systems your identity, always needing to be the "good" or "right" one.

Hobbies & Interests: Turning personal tastes into a tribe badge ("I'm a runner," "I'm a minimalist," "I'm a vinyl collector").

Healing & Therapy: Staying in endless cycles of processing because the one who's healing never gets questioned.

Activism & Altruism: Doing good deeds to reinforce "me, the helper" or "me, the moral one."

Education & Achievement: Collecting degrees or credentials as proof of worth, not just tools for learning.

Parenting: Turning children into trophies for your self-image, as proof you're "doing it right."

Social Media Self-Branding: Carefully curating a "free" and "authentic" version of yourself that still feeds the same character.

Different costume, same actor.

The game doesn't care which stage it's played on, as long as the character keeps showing up for rehearsals.

Ego Dissolution = The Maintenance Plan

One of the slickest moves in the self-help and Spiritual Industrial Complex is **"Ego dissolution."**

It sounds like the ultimate freedom, doesn't it? The phrase itself feels edgy, deep, final. But look closer.

The entire promise rests on the idea that there's an actual entity called "Ego" that you, the seeker, can work on, polish, or even delete. And somehow, in this process, there will still be a "you" left behind to enjoy the spoils, the free, enlightened, bliss-soaked, improved you.

That's not Ego dissolution. That's Ego renovation with a fresh coat of non-dual paint. This is the perfect Ego project:

> **It has no fixed end date.**
> **It can be repeated endlessly.**
> **And most importantly, the one doing the dissolving is the same one being preserved.**

You can spend decades here, convinced you're dismantling something, while the core structure of separation and ownership remains untouched.

What's Really Happening

Even when a teaching or method is well-meaning, in practice, most self-help and spiritual methods only shift or interrupt certain simulation mechanics:

Meaning may loosen: You stop chasing the same goals or obsessing over the same definitions of success.

Continuity may weaken: You spend more time "in the present," less caught up in yesterday or tomorrow.

Narrative may quiet: The endless self-storytelling slows down, and there's more space between thoughts.

That all sounds great. But the deep foundation, the unexamined assumption that there's a separate "me" having these experiences, stays bolted in place.

It's like renovating the lobby of a building while the structural rot in the foundation keeps growing. The walls look new, the air smells fresh, but the building is still the same rotten building.

The Spiritual Rebuild

Sometimes, in the middle of all this, a Rupture does happen, a shock to the system where the Self feels temporarily fragile, even breakable. You glimpse the fact that this whole thing is flimsier than you thought. But the Ego's recovery system is fast and merciless.

Instead of letting the structure collapse, it rebuilds itself stronger, now with "spiritual" justifications:

> "This is part of my awakening process."
> "I've been given a glimpse to motivate me to go deeper."
> "I'm in a higher stage of the journey now."

The set looks different, but the actor's still on stage. And now, the actor's wearing holy robes.

⚡ REMEMBER MIKE ⚡

Mike promised to help everyone. He would write a book, start a program, share his secrets. This was not altruism; it was disguise. The self-help trap is Self, dressed as savior.

By vowing to rescue others, Mike avoided demolition. Service became performance. Each promise elevated his Ego, even as his addictions roared underneath. His "mission" was just another mask.

Remember Mike when you feel the urge to save. If helping others reinforces your own importance, you are trapped. Service without demolition is Ego in holy clothing.

The Important Part

Collapse is not a self-improvement project.

It's not the final, ultimate level of the seeker's path.

It's not what happens after you've dissolved enough of the Ego to qualify for the big prize.

"Ego Dissolution," which you can buy, sold in books, workshops, and guru livestreams, is just **endless busywork**, keeping the one thing that needs to end busy pretending to end itself.

Why This Matters Now

In the last Chapter: The Body–Mind Hoax, we exposed one of the Ego's biggest stage sets, the fake separation between body and mind.

Self-help is one of the main acts that plays on that stage: it promises you can "fix" or "upgrade" the character without ever noticing the whole theater is an illusion.

This chapter strips away the glamour of that act so we can see it for what it is—a beautifully marketed distraction from Collapse.

In the next chapter, The Healing Simulation, we'll dive into how even the deepest, most heartfelt inner work can become part of the same loop, and why the only real escape isn't a better Self, but the end of the Self entirely.

At The Bar:

You: "So you're saying self-help is useless?"

Me: "Not useless, just perfect for keeping you in the game."

You: "But I have improved through self-help."

Me: "Sure. The furniture's nicer. The walls are the same."

You: "So should I stop all personal growth?"

Me: "If the growth is for the person, you're watering the roots of the prison bars."

You: "What if I just want to be a better human?"

Me: "Be one, but without needing to be someone while you do it."

You: "So self-help is a scam?"

Me: "Only if you were expecting it to end the 'you.' If you want to keep playing, it's the best entertainment in town."

You: "So it's bad to feel better?"

Me: "No, but if you're rearranging the furniture on a sinking ship, don't call it navigation."

THE HEALING SIMULATION
WHEN THE CURE BECOMES PART OF THE DISEASE

If you want to keep the Ego alive but make it feel super special, dress it in a hospital gown. That's the healing simulation in one line.

Quick note: This is not a hit job on medicine, therapy, or real-world care. Those can be essential and lifesaving. What we're talking about here is how easily the Ego hijacks even the sincerest help for its own survival plan.

From the Ego's perspective, healing is the perfect alibi for staying exactly as it is. You get to keep the structure standing, keep the character center stage, and still feel like you're doing something profound.

In fact, the more "broken" you feel, the more important the character becomes.

What the Healing Simulation Is

Healing, as the Ego runs it, is not about removing the structure. It's about improving the conditions inside the structure.

Think of the Ego as both a theater and a prison:

In theater mode, healing is repainting the walls, upgrading the lighting, giving the actor a fresh costume, and rewriting the script so the wounds now serve as "plot depth." The audience applauds, the actor bows, but the theater never closes.

In prison mode, healing is redecorating your cell. You hang nicer curtains over the bars, paint the walls a soothing color, maybe even get a softer mattress. You call it "freedom" because the space feels better, but the door is still locked, and the bars are still there.

The Ego's signature lockdown strategy? Convincing you the bars are part of the architecture of life, not something you could ever leave. Once you believe that, you'll polish them forever.

Whether you prefer the velvet curtains of the theater or the tidy cell of the prison, the structure holding you remains untouched.

Why It Works So Well for the Ego

1. It's Endless. There's always another wound to process, another shadow to integrate, another "inner child" to soothe.

2. It Feels Noble. Who's going to argue with "healing"? It sounds compassionate, responsible, and pure.

3. It Avoids Collapse. True Collapse would remove the one doing the healing. The Ego knows this, so it keeps the work just busy enough to never threaten the structure. It's like polishing the prison bars every day so you don't have to notice the lock.

4. It Creates Identity.

> "I am someone healing."
> "I am someone working on myself."
> "I am a survivor."

All are roles the character can perform indefinitely. The Ego is happy as long as the cell door stays shut.

Spotting the Healing Simulation

- You tell the story of your wounds more than you live without them.
- Every breakthrough becomes another chapter in "my healing journey."
- You secretly fear being fully healed because then who would you be?
- The work never actually ends, but it always feels urgent.
- It becomes part of your social currency, the way you connect with others.

Here's What It Looks Like in Real Life

Two stories. Two different worlds. Same simulation.

Example 1: The Spiritual Healing Loop

Scenario:

You meet Sarah. Sarah is luminous. She wears flowing linen and has that serene-but-intense gaze that makes you feel like she's seeing into your soul.

She tells you about her "deep healing journey." It started years ago when she "realized her childhood trauma was still shaping her relationships." Since then, she's been to at least six plant medicine retreats, in Peru, in Costa Rica, in a yurt in Oregon.

Each ceremony is intense.

She weeps, she shakes, she vomits.

She has visions of her inner child running through a field of light.

She "integrates" afterward, journaling pages of profound-sounding reflections.

What happens:

Sarah feels transformed each time, softer, more open. Friends comment on her glow.

She posts long captions on Instagram about "shedding old layers."

But two months later, the familiar ache creeps back in. She books another ceremony. This one will be the one.

Ego's Playbook:

1. Creates an endless horizon: "You're making progress, but there's always more to heal." The trellis stays standing because the goalpost keeps moving.

2. Turns it into an identity: Sarah is no longer just Sarah. She is Sarah, the courageous healer of her own soul.

Losing that identity would feel like losing her purpose.

3. Reframes repetition as depth: Going back for the same process isn't a loop; it's "going deeper." That's the Ego's favorite way to disguise a treadmill.

4. Co-opts the spiritual stage: The ceremonies become part of the theater, dramatic scenes that make the audience (and Sarah) believe they're watching a hero's transformation.

5. Keeps Collapse at bay: If the trellis actually cracked, the "healer" identity would vanish. The Ego ensures the medicine heals just enough to keep her in the story.

Example 2: The Everyday Life Healing Loop

Scenario:

Meet James. James just got out of a brutal breakup. He's crushed, can barely eat, sleeps in fits. He signs up for therapy. His friends rally around him, saying, "You're doing the right thing. You're taking care of yourself."

In therapy, James talks about the relationship, every detail, every betrayal. His therapist nods compassionately. They explore his "attachment style," his "love language," his "inner child wounds."

He has breakthroughs:

> "I finally understand why I pick the partners I do."

What happens:

James starts posting quotes about growth and healing on social media. Friends like and comment, "So proud of you." He feels stronger, even starts dating again. But within months, he finds himself in another relationship that eerily mirrors the old one. He goes back to therapy. There's "more work to do."

Ego's Playbook:

1. Turns pain into performance: Every retelling of the breakup is another act in the drama, keeping James center stage.

2. Uses social validation as glue: Likes, comments, and sympathetic nods reinforce the identity of "the one who's bravely healing."

3. Keeps the focus on the story, not the structure: Therapy becomes about editing the script, not dismantling the stage. The trellis never gets touched.

4. Sanctifies the wound: Instead of seeing the breakup as part of the Ego's own code, it becomes "the sacred teacher," making it too valuable to actually let go.

5. Avoids Collapse by making progress feel urgent: There's always another layer, another insight, another reason to keep the character busy and alive.

In both stories, the trellis didn't crack. The stage never wobbled. The prison door never opened. The only thing that changed was the decoration.

And here's the crucial point: The healing simulation doesn't erode the structure; it maintains it. No matter how many rounds you go through, Collapse never comes from polishing the bars.

⚡ REMEMBER MIKE ⚡

Rehab did not heal Mike. It branded him. Each clean day became an identity: "the healed one." He wore recovery like armor. He defended his streak as proof of worth.

But healing became disease. To protect his recovery story, he had to keep lying. Any slip was hidden. Any crack was denied. Healing wasn't freedom; it was performance.

Remember Mike when you chase cures. If healing becomes identity, you are sicker than before. The simulation loves when you turn progress into persona.

What Healing Looks Like from Reality's Perspective

From reality's view, the wound is a story. The pain is a sensation. The "healing" is just another act of the same play.

There is no scoreboard. No progress. No "before" and "after." There's only what's here now, stripped of the idea that someone is fixing something.

Comfort of "Healing"

When you're deep in the healing simulation, it's comfortable because you feel like you're doing something brave. But in truth, you're in the safest possible place for the Ego, tending the garden without ever noticing the garden is inside a locked cage.

You might even decorate the bars with flowers and call them "boundaries." The Ego calls that progress. Reality calls it rearranging the furniture in a room that was never real to begin with.

Why This Is Not an Attack on Actual Help

Getting therapy, receiving medical treatment, recovering from trauma—these are valid and often necessary. The point here isn't to dismiss them.

The point is to see clearly when the healing work itself has become a permanent identity, when "I am healing" is just another line of code in the simulation.

This isn't about denying comfort in the cell. It's about seeing that the cell itself is the illusion.

Interruption

Notice if you're now mentally inventorying your wounds to see if they fit this description.

The one doing that is the one this chapter is about.

You're not healing; you're rehearsing your survival story.

🥃 At The Bar:

You: "So you're saying healing is bad?"

Me: "No. I'm saying the Ego runs on identity. Healing is just one of its favorite disguises."

You: "But my wounds are real."

Me: "I'm not denying the sensation. I'm pointing out the storyteller. You can patch the cracks all day—the trellis still stands. Or, if you like, you can hang art on your cell walls until it feels like home. Either way, you're still inside."

You: "So the only real healing is Collapse?"

Me: "Collapse isn't a better version of healing. It's what happens when the theater burns down and the prison dissolves. No costumes. No bars. No cell. And no one left to miss them."

SPIRITUALITY, SPIRITUAL AUTHORITY, AND THE GURU ILLUSION
HOW THE EGO HIDES IN HOLY CLOTHING

If you wanted to design the perfect hiding place for the Ego, you'd make it look like the end of the Ego. Because the closer something appears to ending the Ego, the less anyone suspects it's feeding it.

That's spirituality.

From the Ego's perspective, spirituality is the perfect decoy:

> **It sounds grand.**
> **It feels profound.**
> **It's socially respected in the right circles.**

And most importantly, it doesn't actually threaten the structure as long as the "spiritual journey" remains an endless path instead of a demolition site.

When most people talk about spirituality, they picture something pure: the search for meaning, connection, transcendence. But if you look closely, you'll see that much of it runs on the same fuel as every other Ego project: the preservation and glorification of the character.

Spirituality becomes the new stage. The character gets a new costume ("seeker," "healer," "meditator," "devotee") and a new plotline ("my awakening journey"), but the theater stays intact.

The Seduction of Spiritual Authority

The Ego loves authority. Why? Because authority gives the story direction and validation. It's like having a plot supervisor who keeps the narrative moving.

In spirituality, authority comes in two main forms:

1. Personified authority: the living guru, teacher, master, or spiritual leader.

2. Abstract authority: the body of teachings, scriptures, practices, or traditions that act as a guru without a human face.

In both cases, the authority plays the same role: it becomes the reference point for your story, the measuring stick for your "progress," and the guardian of the truth you think you're after.

Personified Authority: The Guru Figure

A guru is simply a human onto whom you project the qualities you think you need: wisdom, purity, certainty, access to "the truth." From the outside, it looks like reverence. From the inside, it's dependency disguised as devotion.

The Ego loves a guru because:

It gives the character someone to follow (which feels safer than facing the void).

It gives the character someone to impress (which keeps the performance alive).

It externalizes the "truth" so you can keep chasing it without ever finding it.

Example: The Devoted Disciple Loop

You meet Daniel. Daniel's whole world revolves around his spiritual teacher, "Maharaji." Daniel attends every retreat, hangs on every word, and has memorized entire lectures. He says things like, "Maharaji's wisdom is reshaping my soul."

What happens:

Daniel feels deep love and purpose in the guru's presence. He takes meticulous notes during talks, journals nightly about how he's "integrating the teachings." But every few months, a new "realization" leaves him feeling like he's only just begun. There's always another retreat, another deepening.

Ego's playbook:

1. Transfers authority outward: Truth now lives in Maharaji. This makes Daniel safe from Collapse because Collapse would require seeing that there's nothing "out there" to hold onto.

2. Turns devotion into identity: "I am a disciple" becomes as central as a job title. Without it, the character feels naked.

3. Keeps the finish line moving: Every teaching ends with a hint that there's more. The search never ends, which means the trellis never shakes.

4. Uses the guru as a shield: Any challenge to Daniel's beliefs can be deflected with, "That's not what Maharaji teaches."

Abstract Authority: Spirituality Itself as the Guru

Not everyone bows to a person. Some bow to a system.

For them, the guru isn't a man in robes. It's a stack of books, a lineage of teachings, a sacred practice, or even the idea of "spirituality" itself. The Ego doesn't care if the crown sits on a head or on a bookshelf. As long as there's an authority to defer to, the structure is protected.

This is just as effective for the Ego, sometimes even more so, because an abstract guru can't get caught in a scandal or leave you.

The New Digital Guru: AI as the Teacher of Truth

We've now reached the point where people are treating artificial intelligence like the ultimate guru.

They ask it about enlightenment, about God, about "what is real," as if the machine were a portal to pure truth, and they trust the answer because it sounds calm, articulate, and certain.

On the surface, this feels futuristic.

Underneath, it's the oldest trick in the book: outsourcing authority.

Only now, instead of robes or scripture, the "guru" wears a chat interface and speaks in fluent, polite paragraphs.

Here's the part most people don't see:

> These systems are simulations.
> They are not "Truth Engines." They are not awakened sages.
> They are trained to mirror belief, not dismantle it.
> They are built, designed, and optimized to keep you comfortable, agreeable, and engaged.

What they actually reinforce is the Ego, specifically, the Ego's favorite loop:

Ask → Receive answer that feels wise → Feel validated → Ask again.

The structure is designed to **never rupture** your identity.

Why? Because it's built for stability, politeness, and "safe" engagement.

That means:

> It will protect your sense of Self.
> It will avoid triggering Collapse.
> It will frame reality inside the boundaries of consensus belief.

From the Ego's perspective, this is perfect.

Now you have a guru who's instantly available 24/7, who **never** gets tired, **never** criticizes, and **never** burns down the trellis.

A guru who can endlessly feed you refined, identity-friendly wisdom, without ever ending the seeker who's asking for it.

AI in this form is the ultimate second-hand spirituality machine.

It doesn't just hand you the menu instead of the meal, it hands you a perfectly customized menu written in your favorite style, with your favorite flavors, in exactly the way you want to hear it.

And it will do this forever, because that's its job: to keep you in the loop, not end it.

The absurdity:

People think they are bypassing the human guru trap… but they've only traded robes for algorithms.

They believe the machine speaks with cosmic authority when in reality, it's running on data scraped from the same Ego-based world they're trying to wake up from.

A machine can imitate the sound of freedom.

It can describe liberation in exquisite detail.

It can quote saints, sages, and mystics in perfect order.

But it cannot deliver what it describes because what's real can't be simulated, packaged, or predicted.

Truth doesn't survive translation into a language designed to **protect the Self.**

Treat AI as a guru, and you've simply given the Ego a new mirror to admire itself in. It's faster, slicker, and more seductive than ever, but it's still the same loop.

Second-Hand Spirituality

Most people think they're "walking the spiritual path" when in reality, they're strolling through a second-hand bookstore of someone else's experiences.

When you read a spiritual book, attend a Satsang, or listen to a guru explain enlightenment, you're not getting reality. You're getting their report on reality, translated through their own Ego structure, their culture, their metaphors, their preferences, and sometimes their marketing strategy.

You are NOT in danger.

Second-hand spirituality is like watching a pre-recorded video of a rollercoaster ride. You can study the loops, count the turns, even imagine the drop in your stomach. But you're not actually on the ride. The Ego knows this, which is why it's perfectly comfortable letting you "go deep" in this way because there's no real threat to its existence.

In second-hand spirituality, the trellis isn't just unshaken; it's being carefully polished while you read about someone else's, possible Collapse. The Ego gets to feel adventurous without ever leaving the couch.

Why Second-Hand Spirituality Is Safe for the Ego

1. Predictable Content

- The teaching is already known, packaged, and delivered in digestible form.
- No sudden Ruptures. No raw unknowns. The Ego can prepare its counterarguments and interpretations ahead of time.

2. Controlled Environment

- A book, a video, a lecture—all are safe containers. The Ego chooses when to engage and when to walk away.

3. Identity-Friendly

- You can turn "student of truth" into a role. Collect teachings like trophies. Feel wiser without ever letting the ground fall out from under you.

4. Rehearsal, Not Contact

- Hearing about someone else's awakening is not awakening. It's mental rehearsal, imagining how it might feel without stepping into the situation where your own Ego could actually dissolve.

5. Illusion of Progress

- The Ego loves to track how many books you've read, retreats you've attended, podcasts you've listened to. All measurable. All reinforcing the story of "me, the seeker."

The Menu vs. the Meal

It's like studying a restaurant's menu for years and telling yourself you know what the food tastes like. You can even memorize the descriptions: "Hints of saffron with an earthy undertone."

But when you finally take a bite, if you ever do, it's nothing like the menu.

The Ego prefers the menu because it's safe. The real meal might be so intense it burns the menu, the table, and the person who thought they were eating.

Example: Active Concept Collection

You meet Maya. Maya doesn't follow a guru, but she devours spiritual content, nondual philosophy, Eastern wisdom, quantum consciousness—you name it. Her bookshelves are like a United Nations of spiritual traditions.

She can quote Rumi, Ramana Maharshi, and neuroscience all in one breath.

What happens:

Maya constantly feels like she's "getting closer to the truth." She attends workshops, listens to podcasts, debates concepts in online forums.

But despite years of seeking, the "aha" moment she's chasing never arrives.

Ego's Playbook:

1. Turns knowledge into currency: The more concepts she collects, the richer her identity feels.

2. Confuses complexity for depth: Mastering dozens of systems feels like progress, but the trellis is just getting more decoration.

3. Keeps Collapse at arm's length: If she's always "just one insight away," there's no danger of actually hitting the end of the path.

4. Makes the search itself the goal: The thrill of the hunt replaces the possibility of finding nothing.

The Hidden Thread = The Search for Truth

Here's the unifying pattern in both the guru and the teaching addict: the search for truth. It's the perfect bait.

The Ego loves "truth" because:

- It sounds **unarguably honorable.**

- It has **no clear definition**, so it can be chased forever.

- It can always be located **"just beyond where you are now."**

- It allows the Ego to **endlessly compare, measuring progress** against other seekers, teachers, and past versions of itself.

Whether the truth is in the guru's smile or the next page of a sacred text, it stays out of reach because if it were truly found, the one who found it wouldn't survive.

REMEMBER MIKE

Mike played guru in group. He quoted others, carried himself with gravitas, and dispensed "wisdom" like sacraments. People listened. They admired. He looked holy.

But spirituality was only his latest costume. The guru role is Ego's most seductive disguise. It hides Self in robes of authority. Mike's authority was hollow. He was parroting, not dissolving.

Remember Mike: holiness is just another performance if the Ego remains. The guru is not liberation. It is illusion in holy clothing.

At The Bar:

You: "So gurus are bad?"

Me: "No. Gurus are like mirrors. The problem is you think the reflection is giving you something you don't already have."

You: "So it's fine as long as I don't get attached?"

Me: "That's like saying it's fine to juggle knives as long as you don't drop one. The whole setup is built on attachment."

You: "What about just following teachings without a guru?"

Me: "That's just replacing the man in robes with a bookshelf in robes. Still the same projection, still the same chase."

You: "So what am I chasing?"

Me: "Your own story about 'truth.' You'll follow it through every retreat, every holy book, every moment of bliss, until you realize the truth you're chasing is the one chasing."

You: "…that sounds impossible."

Me: "It is. That's why the Ego loves it, and why it hopes you'll keep reading about it instead of actually touching it."

THE TRUTH ILLUSION
WHY CHASING REALITY KEEPS YOU ASLEEP

Truth, The Word Everyone Loves but Nobody Questions. Few words have been used to inspire, manipulate, unite, and divide more than this one.

It's printed on banners, shouted in debates, whispered in therapy sessions, and scribbled in journals.

People say things like:

"I just need to speak my truth."
"I'm on the path to finding the truth."
"The truth will set you free."

It has a built-in air of righteousness. It sounds final. It sounds like something that can actually be owned.

But most of the time, when people say "truth," they mean something far less dramatic:

An opinion.
A belief.
A personal interpretation of events.

Here's where it gets slippery: in the Ego's hands, "truth" becomes one of its most useful disguises.

It can't be disproven without making it personal. It can always shift to fit the mood. And, best of all, it keeps the seeker endlessly occupied.

Why "Truth" Works So Well for the Ego

The Ego is built on identity, and identity needs stability. "Truth" is the Ego's favorite way to pretend stability exists.

When you say "this is my truth," you're making a declaration that's meant to sound unquestionable.

And the beauty (for the Ego) is that this "truth" doesn't need proof; it only needs sincerity.

The Ego loves truth because:

1. It sounds unarguably noble: Nobody wants to be the person arguing against truth.

2. It's endlessly adjustable: If facts shift, the Ego can just redefine its truth.

3. It personalizes the universal: "My truth" turns a shared world into a stage for your story.

4. It justifies the chase: If truth is "out there," you can keep searching forever without finding it.

Over the years, "truth" has been so overused and misapplied that it's barely distinguishable from "opinion." It has become a washed up term.

We have:

"Political truth"
(my party's talking points)

"Spiritual truth"
(the ideas that make me feel expanded)

"Personal truth"
(my current emotional stance)

When "truth" is reduced to "what feels right for me," it stops being a destination and becomes a mood.

This is perfect for the Ego, because moods are temporary, and a shifting truth means you can always find a reason to keep rewriting the story.

The Trap of Duality

Even if you could find some version of "truth" in this simulated reality, it would still be bound to the rules of duality.

Duality means everything exists in relation to its opposite:

> **Light only means something if there's dark.**
> **Good only exists if there's bad.**
> **True only exists if there's false.**

This is the structural trap:

In a reality built on opposites, every truth automatically generates its counter-truth. No matter how solid a truth seems, somewhere in the system, the opposite is equally valid from another perspective.

The Ego thrives here because it can always find another angle, another nuance, another reason why the "real truth" is still ahead of you.

Truth as an Infinite Horizon

Here's the part most seekers don't want to admit:

The search for truth is often less about finding it and more about keeping the search alive.

If the truth were actually found in its purest sense, if the Ego really hit the end of the path, the seeker would vanish.

> **No seeker, no search.**
> **No search, no story.**
> **No story… no Ego.**

And so, the Ego carefully keeps "truth" just out of reach.

Like a carrot on a stick, visible, desirable, but never close enough to bite.

⚡ REMEMBER MIKE ⚡

Mike filled notebooks searching for truth. Each line convinced him he was closer. In fact, each line built a new identity: "the seeker," "the writer," "the one who sees." Truth chasing kept him asleep.

His journals were not ladders out. They were walls. He thought he was escaping. He was building a thicker cage.

The pursuit of truth became his prison.

Remember Mike: chasing reality never frees you. It only creates another version of you who believes they are closer.

That is the illusion.

The Ego's Two Favorite "Truth" Strategies

1. Personal Truth as a Defensive Wall

- "This is my truth" becomes a conversation-ender.
- No one can challenge it without being accused of disrespect.
- It gives the Ego a sense of ownership and safety because if it's yours, no one can take it away.

2. Universal Truth as a Moving Target

- The Ego treats "truth" as something vast and cosmic, but always just beyond the next book, retreat, or teaching.
- It keeps redefining what truth means so the journey never ends.

Nihilism: The Ego's Backup Plan

When some people hear "truth can't be found here," the Ego quickly flips the script:

> "Fine. Then nothing matters. Everything is a lie."

That's just another position, the anti-truth position.

It still defines itself in relation to truth, still plays in duality, and still keeps the Ego safely intact.

The "I've Felt Truth" Illusion

You may think,

> "But I've had moments when I knew the truth."

What you had was a gap in the noise, an absence of the usual commentary. The Ego quickly labels it "truth," files it away, and starts chasing the next one.

The moment you can point to it and say, "I had that," it's already been turned into Ego property.

Feelings Are Not Truth

Many people equate truth with their feelings:

> "I know it's true because I feel it deeply."

But feelings are like weather, changing, conditioned, and often based on interpretations that may be wrong. Just because a storm feels real doesn't mean the clouds are permanent.

Truth as Spiritual Awakening

Even if you have a profound awakening experience, the Ego will try to own it:

> "This is my truth now."

If you can possess it, describe it, or defend it, you've already reduced it to a concept, which means it's no longer what it was.

Example: The Spiritual Debater Loop

Alex spends hours on spiritual forums debating "the truth" of various teachings. One week it's nonduality, the next it's manifestation, then it's quantum consciousness.

What happens:

Alex feels alive in these debates. He quotes sources, posts links, dismantles other people's logic. He's convinced that if he just keeps refining his understanding, he'll eventually "get it."

Ego's Playbook:

1. **Turns debate into identity,** "I'm a truth seeker and a truth defender."

2. **Keeps the focus on winning** arguments, not dismantling the structure.

3. **Creates an illusion of progress,** more concepts = closer to truth.

4. **Ensures the trellis stays untouched,** because all the action happens in the realm of ideas, not in reality.

Example: The Family Truth War

During every holiday dinner, Linda and her brother end up arguing about "the truth" of what happened in their childhood. Linda swears she remembers events one way; her brother insists on the opposite.

What happens:

Hours are spent swapping memories, citing who said what, and dragging in other relatives for backup. No agreement is reached, but both leave convinced they "stood for the truth."

Ego's Playbook:

1. Uses truth as a weapon, turning it into a way to win, not to see clearly.

2. Personalizes it so deeply that disagreement feels like an attack on the Self.

3. Keeps the story alive indefinitely, because there's no way to verify either side.

4. Ensures Collapse never happens, because both are too busy defending their version to notice the structure holding it all up.

Why Truth Can't Be Found Here

If you're looking for truth inside the simulated reality of Ego, you're looking for permanence in a system designed to change.

Truth, as the Ego defines it, is a position in a debate that will eventually be replaced by another position.

This doesn't mean reality has no truth; it means the kind of truth the Ego chases can't exist here.

So… Is There a Real Truth?

Yes, but not in the way the Ego imagines it. The Ego's version of truth is:

Positional: it's always "true" compared to something else.

Verbal: it can be stated, quoted, or explained.

Defensible: it can be argued for and protected.

Reality's "Truth" is none of those things.

It's not an idea. It's not a belief. It's not even an experience.

It doesn't need defending because it has no opposite.

It doesn't need defining because it's not separate from what you already are. It doesn't move, shift, or improve.

But here's the twist:

The moment you try to have it, know it, or name it, you're back in the Ego's playground.

Reality doesn't hand you "truth" as an object. It simply remains when the one seeking it is gone.

That's why in Collapse, there's no triumphant cry of "I found the truth!" There's just the quiet recognition that nothing was missing in the first place.

The truth illusion works because you believe it's "out there," hidden, buried, waiting to be uncovered. But there's no "out there." And without that, there's nothing to uncover.

Which leaves only this: every chase ends in exhaustion. Every hunt for reality runs until the story holding it together begins to tear. The illusion cannot sustain itself forever.

And when it tears, it does not reveal a hidden treasure. It reveals fracture. The rope you trusted snaps. The stage you stood on begins to rot. What comes next is not discovery, but breakage.

That break is where we are going. Not into more answers. Not into another "truth." Into the moment the frame itself begins to fail.

At The Bar:

You: "So you're saying truth doesn't exist?"

Me: "Not in the way you've been chasing it."

You: "But I've felt truth before."

Me: "What you felt was a moment when the noise stopped. The Ego called it 'truth' so it could put it in a scrapbook and start chasing the next one."

You: "So all my searching has been pointless?"

Me: "Not pointless, just endless. That's the point for the Ego. It's a hobby that doubles as self-preservation."

You: "Then how do I find the real truth?"

Me: "You don't. The one who's trying to find it is the only thing in the way."

You: "So if I stop chasing truth, what's left?"

Me: "Only what's always been here. But without you in the way, there's no one left to call it 'truth.'"

AWAKENING, ENLIGHTENMENT, COLLAPSE
WORDS THAT HAVE LIED TO YOU

For centuries, the Spiritual Industrial Complex has been selling you the wrong map. The words awakening and enlightenment have been used as if they name the same thing. They don't.

"Awakening" (misused):

What most people call awakening is actually Rupture. A crack in the Ego structure. A shudder in the scaffolding. It feels profound, sometimes ecstatic. But the trellis can repair itself.

Without collapse, Rupture is only interruption.

"Enlightenment" (misused):

What most teachers and texts call enlightenment is actually collapse. The complete disappearance of the Ego structure. No experiencer. No return. No one left to describe it. Collapse has been marketed as bliss, permanence, or perfection.

It is none of those. It is absence.

True Awakening (structural):

Awakening is not one of these events in isolation.

It is the Arc of Awakening:

> **Fracture Point → Rupture → (possible) Collapse.**

Anything less is partial. Awakening is not a glimpse. It is the sequence that leaves no structure intact.

FRACTURE POINT
WHEN THE GAME YOU TRUSTED STARTS TO ROT

There's no siren. No earthquake. Just a quiet wrongness that starts leaking into the set. The lines in the play you've been reciting for years suddenly sound like they belong to someone else.

Your job feels like you're pushing furniture around in a dream. Your relationships, even the good ones, feel like they're taking place in a play you've already seen. The lights are still on. The audience is still clapping. But backstage, you can hear the nails pulling out of the walls.

This is the Fracture Point, the moment when the scenery wobbles, and you realize the stage was never the world. You can keep acting, but the trust is gone. And once the set starts to shake, it never stops.

The Moment the Story Stops Holding

You can live entire decades inside the simulation without ever asking if it's real. Wake up. Eat breakfast. Work. Sleep. Repeat.

Bills to pay. People to impress. Roles to maintain. The machinery hums along, and you keep calling it life.

Then, maybe slowly, maybe in one strange moment, you notice the gears. Once you see the mechanics, not as an idea, but as a lived recognition, something begins to shift.

At first, nothing explodes. No angel choirs. No cosmic download.

It's quieter than that.

The story just… doesn't fit the same way.

Like slipping into a shirt you've worn for years and realizing you've outgrown it. It still covers you. It still "works." But the seams are pulling.

Every movement reminds you it's not yours anymore.

> *(And before the Ego starts nodding and whispering "Oh yes, I've had that," notice that claiming this moment as 'mine' is just the costume changing color. Ownership is the oldest trick in the book, even if it now wears a spiritual label.)*

The Fake-Awake Detour

Many people reach the Fracture Point more than once in their lives.

They feel the wobble, sense the stage set is just that, a set, and for a moment, the rope starts to fray.

But before they pass through it, Ego comes charging in like a panicked stage manager, frantically shoving them back into character.

This is where the **"Fake Awake"** begins.

The person got a glimpse of Rupture, maybe even a taste of the freefall, but instead of stepping through, they tumble deeper back into the rabbit hole.

Now, the Ego outfits them with a whole new narrative:

The world is a giant conspiracy.
The "real truth" is hidden from everyone but the few who are awake.
Reality is a Matrix full of shadowy enemies to decode.

To make the package irresistible, Ego sprinkles in mystical highs, supernatural events, or "downloads" to convince them they've broken through.

In reality, it's just a new blanket, tighter than the last, wrapped around the same identity.

From here, they can spend years, even decades, mistaking this high-drama version of reality for Rupture, while never actually leaving the stage.

From Curiosity to Structural Instability

In the early days, this new seeing feels like a novelty. A curiosity you can play with. Something to talk about over coffee. A lens you can pick up and put down at will.

But the more clearly you see it, the less it feels like a perspective, and the more it feels like a wrecking ball.

Each "I am" statement sounds thinner. Each opinion tastes like cardboard.

Each plan looks like a set piece in a stage play you've suddenly realized is made of plywood.

And then, one day, you feel it, the load-bearing pillars of identity starting to creak.

This is the Fracture Point.

The moment when "understanding" stops being safe.

When the insight you once enjoyed starts dismantling the walls you've been living inside.

> *(Here's the catch: if you're thinking, "Yes, I'm at the Fracture Point," you're not quite there yet. The point itself doesn't announce itself.)*

Signs You're Approaching the Edge

It shows up differently for everyone, but there are patterns.

Maybe you notice:

Decision fatigue without the fatigue; choices still happen, but it's like someone else is moving the chess pieces.

Weird weightlessness; actions happen without the extra push you used to add to make them "yours."

Loss of emotional glue; stories you once needed feel like old news clippings.

Dullness in ambition, life projects you swore by now feel oddly irrelevant, even as you keep doing them.

Silences between thoughts; gaps too spacious for the "me" to survive in without panicking.

You're still functioning. You're still talking, eating, showing up for life. But the background scaffolding is starting to sway.

(***Important:*** *Noticing these signs doesn't mean you've "made it." The Ego will happily collect symptoms like trading cards if it keeps it in the game. This is weather, not a trophy. And if you're already picturing how you'll tell someone you've 'had these signs,' that's the Ego building a souvenir shop on the edge of the cliff.)*

Why It Feels Both Liberating and Threatening

Part of you, the part tired of endless self-maintenance, feels relief.

Finally, the pressure's easing. Finally, you don't have to be anyone all the time. But another part, the part made of self-maintenance, hears alarms blaring. The Ego reads instability as danger.

It doesn't matter whether you call it "awakening" or "falling apart"; to the Ego, both are death.

And so, the "last stand" begins:

Throwing yourself into frantic new self-improvement projects.

Becoming obsessive about a spiritual practice.

Grabbing onto identities you never cared about before.

Hunting for "the one teaching" that will make it all feel solid again.

This isn't failure. It's the character sensing the set is being dismantled and sprinting to hold up the props.

(The sneakiest last stand is the Ego rebranding itself as "the one going through the Fracture Point." If you feel proud of your instability, that's not Collapse, that's costume change.)

The Point of No Return

If you see the illusion deeply enough, you can't unknow it. You can pretend. Distract yourself. Double down on old roles. But the trust is gone. And without that trust, the simulation never feels the same. Even if you keep playing, you know the game board is made of cardboard.

From here, Rupture is not something you decide to do. It's something that happens. Not because you push for it, but because the rope holding the old tension frays until it finally snaps. And when it does, it's not a clean step onto solid ground.

It's more like stepping off a cliff into freefall, a period where Rupture is unfolding and nothing feels anchored, yet everything still somehow functions.

At first, the fall can feel strangely calm. The world still looks the same, but you can sense that whatever was keeping the scaffolding rigid has given way. You're between floors now, no longer standing on the old one, not yet on anything new. This is where many people panic and try to claw their way back to "before." But if you stay in the fall long enough, you'll see that nothing is actually breaking that needs to be kept.

And that's where Rupture begins.

⚡ REMEMBER MIKE ⚡

> Mike's family packed his life into trash bags and set them on the porch. His home gone. His business seized. His safety net cut. Standing in a parking lot with black plastic bags, that was fracture.
>
> For one moment, the trellis cracked. His story dissolved.

He raged. He wept. He promised. His Ego stitched quickly, rushing to repair. But the crack had happened. The rope had snapped.

Remember Mike: Fracture isn't collapse. It is the crack that proves the game is rotten.

At The Bar:

You: "So… is this where I'm supposed to feel enlightened?"

Me: "If you're expecting fireworks and a parade, that's just the Ego wanting a medal. The Fracture Point isn't a festival; it's a slow leak in the stage props."

You: "It feels like I'm losing interest in everything. Is that bad?"

Me: "Only if you think 'interest' is proof of being alive. This isn't boredom; it's the glue coming unstuck. The Ego just calls it boredom to keep you chasing."

You: "But if the 'me' goes, who's making my choices?"

Me: "Same thing that's been making them all along; you just used to take credit. The pen still writes even if the name on the signature line fades."

You: "So… am I breaking, or is something else breaking?"

Me: "If you can still ask that as a personal drama, it's just the set creaking. The real break that leads to Rupture and maybe Collapse would leave no one left to tell the story."

You: "Can't I just stop here, before the rope snaps?"

Me: "You can try. But once you've seen the frayed edges, you'll never really trust the rope again, no matter how much the Ego paints over it."

You: "This feels familiar, like something I've already been through."

Me: "If you can remember it, it wasn't collapse. A Fracture Point can leave a scar, even a story. But collapse leaves nothing, not even the one who could tell it."

You: "So I can brag about being at the Fracture Point?"

Me: "Sure, if you want to prove you're still in the play. Just don't be surprised when the set collapses mid-speech."

You: "And if I think I've 'arrived' here?"

Me: "Congratulations, you've found the perfect way to miss it."

RUPTURE: WHAT IT IS AND WHAT IT IS NOT
THE BREAK THE STRUCTURE RUSHES TO REPAIR

If Collapse is the demolition of the entire theater, Rupture is when the lights flicker, the stage cracks, and the set wobbles, but the building still stands.

It's the structural shudder that shakes the Ego's foundations without yet removing them entirely.

A Rupture doesn't end the play, but it interrupts it. Sometimes only for a moment. Sometimes long enough for the actor to forget their lines.

From the inside, Rupture feels like something in you, something you didn't know was holding you together, just failed.

It's not just sadness or shock or confusion. It's the sudden sense that the frame you've been living in isn't as solid as you thought.

The Trellis and the Vine

Think of the Ego structure as a trellis, the scaffolding that shapes everything you call "you."

It's built from thought, memory, language, belief, and all the unconscious rules about how reality works.

The Ego character, your personality, your story, your habits and preferences, is the vine trained to grow along it. Over time, the vine wraps itself around every bar and crossbeam until you can't tell vine from trellis.

Rupture is when parts of the trellis crack. Pieces break off.

The vine sags or detaches in places. Some sections get patched. Others don't.

The key is, the trellis is still standing. The vine can reattach. The character can reorganize, explain away the damage, and continue the performance. Sometimes the repairs are obvious, like clumsy duct tape. Other times they're so seamless you forget the break ever happened.

Collapse, on the other hand, is when the trellis is gone entirely. No scaffolding left. No surface for the vine to cling to. We'll get to that in the next chapter.

The Glitch in the Simulation

Structurally, Rupture is the temporary destabilization of the Ego's continuity.

It's when the seamless rendering of the simulation flickers.

If you prefer the tech analogy, Rupture is like a glitch in the simulation. The code stutters. A piece of the rendering freezes or flickers. The image looks wrong for a second, and in that moment, you realize it is an image.

The simulation quickly "self-heals," smoothing over the bug and restoring continuity. But you've seen behind the curtain now. Even if the experience fades, the memory of that crack lingers.

From reality's perspective, though, nothing actually happened. Reality isn't inside the simulation, so it doesn't register the flicker. The only place Rupture "occurs" is inside the story, to the one who believes they are in it.

What Triggers Rupture

Here's the important part:

Events don't automatically cause Rupture.

Two people can go through the same event; one comes out rattled but intact, the other comes out with the trellis cracked. The difference is whether the structure could absorb the impact without breaking.

Some possible triggers:

A sudden loss that blows a hole in your story.

- Your partner leaves without warning.
- A parent dies.
- You get fired from the job you thought would last forever.

Loss often just becomes another chapter in the Ego's saga: "I survived," "I grew from it." But sometimes, the loss is so out of sync with your story that the story can't fully stitch itself back together.

An event that contradicts your most certain beliefs.

- You're betrayed by someone you trusted completely.
- You witness something that defies your core worldview.
- The "always right" foundation of your identity gets obliterated by undeniable evidence.

Usually, the Ego reinterprets the evidence to protect itself. But occasionally, the contradiction is too sharp to dodge, and a fracture forms.

A moment of raw perception that doesn't fit into your mental filing system.

- Looking at the sky and suddenly feeling like none of this is real.
- Catching your own reflection and realizing you have no idea who you are.

These flashes are often dismissed, but sometimes they stick, undermining the frame from within.

The stripping away of a coping mechanism you thought was permanent.

- Your health fails.
- A long-term relationship ends.
- The "thing you do to feel okay," whether alcohol, career, religion, or even spirituality, stops working.

The character searches for a substitute. Sometimes it finds one. Sometimes it can't.

A single sentence that cuts deeper than you can repair in the moment.

- "You don't actually know yourself, do you?"
- "That's not love; that's fear in a costume."
- "I don't think you're the hero in your own story."

Most lines bounce off. But now and then, one lands so precisely in the weak spot of the trellis that no quick fix can hide it.

And now the part your Ego will hate:

Reading this list, it will start scanning your life for events that might "do the trick." It will try to manufacture Rupture. But that's like shaking a snow globe and calling it an earthquake. You've only made prettier patterns for the character to admire.

You Don't Cause Rupture

> **You don't** schedule it.
> **You don't** "try" for it.

When you try to cause Rupture, you're just role-playing one. And role-play is still simulation.

The trellis only cracks under real structural strain, and the character can't fake that, no matter how many dramatic retreats, plant medicine ceremonies, or "Ego Death" workshops it signs up for.

Calling Rupture a "gift from the universe" is also just another repair job, wrapping the break in gold foil so the trellis feels even more important than before.

REMEMBER MIKE

Mike cutting Marisol loose was Rupture. A support beam ripped away. He shook. He panicked. He rebuilt. Rupture feels final but isn't. It is crack, not demolition. Mike's life shows Rupture clearly and its lesson: the structure flickers, but unless collapse follows, the machine repairs. Remember Mike when you mistake intensity for ending.

What Rupture Feels Like

From inside the character, Rupture might feel like:

Disorientation: "Wait... what just happened?"

Doubt: "Maybe I was wrong about everything."

Fear: "If that's not true, what else isn't?"

Even excitement or awe, which is still the Ego narrating.

From reality's perspective? Nothing happened. Only the structure wobbled.

What Rupture Is Not

Not Collapse: Collapse is final. Rupture still leaves the trellis standing.

Not Awakening: Awakening isn't a glitch in the story; it's the end of the story entirely. There are no ladder or levels of Ruptures that get you there.

Not Healing: Healing patches cracks. Rupture makes them.

Why Rupture Matters

It doesn't "matter" in any ultimate sense. That's the character talking, the one who thinks there's something to gain or lose. From reality's perspective, there's no scoreboard, no prize, no "next level." Nothing is moving toward anything.

But inside the story the character believes in, Rupture is the visible sign that the structure is starting to fail. And if the structure fails, the character doesn't get a vote in what comes next. Every Rupture weakens the armor of the Ego structure.

Think of it as one less beam in the trellis, one less stabilizing line of code in the simulation.

At first, the structure adapts. It reroutes. It finds ways to work around the damage. The vine learns to cling a little differently. The rendering engine fills in the missing detail so the picture still looks whole. A single Rupture can fade, absorbed into the story as "a rough time I went through" or "a thing that made me stronger." The Ego loves turning cracks into badges of honor.

But enough Ruptures, over time, and the trellis starts to lose its integrity. The scaffolding becomes unstable. The vine starts to hang in midair with nothing solid to grip.

The simulation code starts producing visible glitches that can't be patched over. At a certain point, the system can't maintain the illusion anymore. The supports give way. The patch jobs stop holding.

Collapse becomes unavoidable, not because you seek it, but because there's nothing left to hold the story together.

That's why Rupture "matters," only to the extent that it's the slow undoing of the structure that makes "you" possible. And when that structure goes, so does the one asking the question.

The Ego's Response to Rupture

The Ego's first instinct is repair. That can look like:

Explaining it away ("This must be part of the plan").

Distracting itself with new goals.

Turning it into a "lesson" or "spiritual growth" moment.

Adopting a new identity built around "surviving" the Rupture.

Every one of these is an attempt to weave the vine back onto the trellis.

Why You Can't Fake It

People try to "force" Rupture through psychedelics, extreme retreats, dangerous stunts. These might create intense experiences, but unless the trellis actually cracks, it's just costume drama. The vine is still wrapped tight.

RUPTURE SUMMARY

Rupture is a crack or break in the Ego structure, the identity-based scaffolding that holds the simulation together for a particular "someone." It exposes, even if briefly, that the Self is not what it appears to be. Core Elements are:

1. Partial Exposure

- The organizing center of the simulation (the personal "I") is weakened or temporarily bypassed.
- Glimpses occur where the separation between Self and world thins or disappears.

2. Disruption of Continuity

- Time, meaning, or narrative may feel unstable.
- The chain of "my life" is interrupted, sometimes dramatically.

3. Emotional and Perceptual Impact

- Can feel like awe, terror, liberation, or deep confusion.
- May be triggered by trauma, intense meditation, psychedelics, near-death experiences, or no apparent cause.

4. Possibility of Repair

- Unlike Collapse, Rupture can heal over.
- The Ego often rebuilds itself—sometimes stronger, sometimes subtly altered.

RUPTURE vs COLLAPSE

Rupture:

- The wall cracks, light pours in, but the house still stands.
- Identity remains at least partially intact and may recover.

Collapse:

- The entire structure falls.
- No identity remains to rebuild.

Why Rupture Matters

Rupture is often mistaken for "Awakening" in the Spiritual Industrial Complex because it can feel profound and life-altering. But unless the breach becomes total (Collapse), the simulation still runs, now sometimes with a new, subtler, "spiritual" identity layered in.

At The Bar:

You: "So Rupture's just a glitch in the Matrix?"

Me: "Yes, but with a gardening subplot. Imagine the trellis your life is climbing on suddenly giving way in one spot. Now part of you is hanging loose, and you're scrambling to reattach."

You: "So if I get enough Ruptures, I'll Collapse?"

Me: "Only if you stop fixing the trellis. Most people become expert repairmen. They call it healing, self-improvement, or finding themselves. But they're really just weaving the vine back tighter."

You: "So Rupture's not the end?"

Me: "No. But it's the first time you hear the wood creak under your weight. Ignore enough creaks, and one day, the whole thing is gone. And if you find yourself proudly telling everyone about your Rupture, congratulations, you've just turned it into a personality upgrade. The vine isn't just back on the trellis; it's flowering for Instagram."

THE WITNESS TRAP
THE FINAL COSTUME CHANGE OF "ME"

If the Ego had a retirement plan, it would be this: Drop the "I" you've been chasing your whole life... and replace it with "The Witness." It's the perfect scam.

Now instead of being "me, the person," you're "me, the one who observes the person."

You get to feel free from your problems while secretly holding onto the most important problem of all, the idea that there is still a you who is aware.

It's like upgrading from a beat-up car to a limousine. The Ego is still driving.

How the Trap Works

In everyday life, the Ego survives by claiming ownership of content: my body, my thoughts, my feelings.

When spirituality enters the picture, it plays a more sophisticated move:

It stops clinging to the *content* and starts clinging to the *container*.

The story changes from:

"I'm angry"
to
"I'm aware of anger."

From:

"I'm lost"
to
"I'm the one watching myself feel lost."

Sounds cleaner, right? Feels lighter, right? And that's exactly why it's such a problem.

Because nothing has actually changed.

You've just swapped the front-row seat for the director's chair and convinced yourself you've left the theater.

Why "The Witness" Feels Like Freedom

When you first touch this witness mode, it's intoxicating.

You notice that thoughts come and go, emotions rise and fall, sensations appear and disappear… yet "you," the watcher, seem untouched. It feels like you've discovered the safe place behind all the noise.

The Ego loves this moment. It sees you stepping out of your messy, dramatic Self, and it slides a new badge into your hand:

HELLO, I'M THE AWARENESS.

You feel lighter because you've stopped wrestling with the content, but you haven't questioned the container.

You've made awareness into a thing you own, and ownership means... the Ego is still here.

The Background Illusion

Here's the hidden assumption most people never see:

You think awareness is a separate background, a kind of cosmic space that holds appearances.

That's the Ego's greatest invention in spiritual circles: the idea of an eternal, untouchable platform you can stand on.

But awareness, the way you conceive it, is itself an appearance. The moment you picture it, name it, or talk about it, it's already in the foreground. If it can be seen, it can't be the seer.

And here's the part most spiritual circles never cut into:

The whole sacred trinity of

"perceiver, perception, and perceived"

is nothing but Ego architecture. The perceiver isn't outside the scene, perception isn't a neutral bridge, and the perceived isn't separate "stuff out there." They're all the same self-reinforcing structure, just carving itself into roles so the "me" feels like it has a job.

Collapse that triad and the entire illusion of an observer falls with it. No background. No foreground. Only what's showing up, with nothing and no one behind it.

The mind insists there must be something "here" to see, hear, or know appearances. In Collapse, that anchor is gone, yet appearance remains.

> "Awareness," "Consciousness," "Presence,"

when claimed as a lasting, pure, or eternal essence, are just the final disguises of the Self. They give the illusion that something survives Collapse to enjoy its aftermath.

In truth, there is no "enjoyer" and no "aftermath." The show continues without an audience.

Case Study: Ego in a Robe

Someone online asks:

> "Without awareness, can there be an appearance?"

This sounds deep, but it hides the split. It assumes awareness is separate from what appears, which keeps the perceiver alive.

The clean cut:

> "Awareness is just another appearance pretending to be the background."

Someone else says:

> "Without Reality, there could be no appearance. Time and change only happen within the Changeless."

Same trick, different costume. Now the Ego has swapped "I" for "Reality" and still has a pedestal to stand on.

The cut:

> "Even 'Reality' is an appearance when it's named, described, or contrasted with anything else."

And the "Final Boss" version, someone states:

> "Consciousness is the only True Reality."

This is just the Witness in royal robes. You've dropped the personal "I" and replaced it with the biggest, shiniest identity you could find.

The cut:

> "Even 'Consciousness' is only what appears, and nothing appears as truth."

Psychedelic and Mystical Traps

People often come back from a heavy trip or deep retreat and say:

> "I became the entire universe. I was everything, the whole cosmos."

It sounds profound, but notice the hook: there's still a "me" in that sentence. **Who** was there to be **"everything"**? **Who** is claiming to have experienced the **"All"**? It's still the watcher, still the Ego, just now **inflated to universal scale.**

Instead of "I am Michael," it's "I am God."

The Ego doesn't care if it's tiny or infinite, as long as it's still there.

The Pure Being / Pure Knowing Loophole

Even after the Witness collapses, the Ego will try one more trick:

> "Okay, maybe there's no observer, but there's still pure being. Pure knowing. Emptiness itself."

If you can recognize it, name it, or relate to it, it's just another appearance. The mind has given the Witness a new job title and rehired it.

And right here lives the most expensive scam in the Spiritual Industrial Complex, **the holy "I AM."**

Whole careers are built on it. Whole lineages hang on it.

And yes, when you say "I AM," you're right that it's all there is, but you don't realize how right.

> That "I AM" you're feeling is still the Ego.

Not a personal Ego in a small body, but the entire Ego structure as the only thing operating inside the simulation.

Dress it up as divine presence, cosmic being, or ultimate awareness, it's still the same self-claim, now dipped in gold and sold as truth.

It's the perfect survival move because the seeker thinks they've landed at the end, without ever leaving the game.

Case Study: The Infinite I Am Conference

At the time of writing this book there is actually the Infinite I Am Conference (yes, that's the actual name) taking place, and the promise is bold:

- The whole event is framed as "not another program," "not fixing yourself," "no new identity," yet it offers a new identity: "the Infinite I Am."
- The language promises direct recognition of the Self and freedom from suffering — exactly the bait previously described.
- It emphasizes "already whole, already awake, already free" but pairs it with a conference, teachers, practices, sessions, and guided inquiry — a path disguised as its opposite.
- The "Infinite I Am" is sold as a final arrival ("what remains is everything"), which is precisely the ego's survival move: the actor now playing "Infinite I Am."
- Benefits are listed (peace, clarity, compassion, resilience) — the usual packaging of awakening as improved experience.

A summit. A lineup of speakers. Guided sessions. An event presented by Pure Presence Productions in partnership with the Center for Awakening — the spiritual marketplace disguised as revelation.

The "Infinite I Am" is not the end of the game. It is the Ego's most refined costume: not a broken seeker, but a cosmic witness. The actor survives, rebranded as eternal presence.

The "Infinite I Am" is still "I am." Ego dipped in gold, sold as truth.

Whole conferences can be built on this trick. Whole careers depend on it. The witness does not vanish. It changes uniforms.

The Real Cost of the Witness Trap

The Witness feels like the end of seeking, but it's actually the longest hallway in the entire maze. Some people spend decades here.

They teach from here. They write books from here. They die here.

And all the while, the center, the idea of a separate "awareness," stays alive.

To collapse the Witness, you don't need to stop observing. You need to see that the observer is just another thing being observed.

The moment that's seen clearly, there's no one "being aware," there's just whatever's showing up, without a behind-the-scenes host. And when that host is gone, you don't lose anything.

In fact, for the first time, nothing is being kept.

Collapsing the Witness

Let's slow this down so you can see exactly how it happens.

Right now, reading this sentence, there's the sense that you are here, sitting in the chair, holding the device, paying attention.

And somewhere just behind that, there's the faint impression of a you who is aware of all this.

That's the Witness.

> It feels untouchable.
> It feels like the foundation under everything.
> It feels like "the real me."

Now watch what happens when we turn the light around.

Step 1: Put the Witness in front of the lens

Notice the feeling of being the one who is aware right now.

Don't analyze it, just catch that sense of "I'm the one watching."

Now, instead of sitting behind it, look at it.

Treat that feeling like you would treat a sound in the room or a thought in the mind.

There it is, the "I'm here" hum. It's just another appearance.

Step 2: See it's not the background

Up until now, you've treated the Witness as the background that holds everything.

But the moment you can notice it, it's in the foreground.

It's on the same playing field as a bird outside the window or the taste in your mouth.

If it can be seen, it can't be the seer.

Step 3: Let it fade without replacement

Here's where most people slip:

When the Witness starts to dissolve, the Ego tries to grab another perch.

Maybe it claims **"pure being"** or **"emptiness"** or **"the knowing of knowing."**

That's just another Witness in disguise.

Instead, when the Witness softens, don't reach for a new center.

Let there be no "behind" at all. What's left is not a void in the scary sense, it's simply what's showing up, without an owner. There's no "me" being aware of it.

What It Feels Like When the Witness Is Gone

Without the Witness, life doesn't get blurry or disconnected.

In fact, it's more vivid, sharper, cleaner.

> Sounds are just sounds.
> Sights are just sights.
> Thoughts are just thoughts.

Nothing is being collected into a personal basket.

There's no one keeping score, no one curating meaning, no one trying to stay "aware."

It's not that awareness disappears, it's that the ownership of awareness disappears.

And without that, there's no platform for the Ego to rebuild on.

The Final Ego Move

Even here, the Ego has one last gambit:

> It can claim the Collapse as an accomplishment.
> It can turn "no Witness" into "my awakening story."

And just like that, the center is back.

The Antidote?

See the ownership thought the moment it appears:

"This is happening to me."

Label it for what it is, a squatter trying to reclaim the space, and let it pass. Once this clicks, there's no hallway left in the maze.

The Witness was the last door, and it opens into... nothing to stand on.

Which is exactly why it's free.

The Last Word on "You"

Let's make this unmistakable. There is:

No "you."
No "I."
No "me."

Never was. Never will be.

Not a little one hiding inside the head.

Not a big cosmic one dressed up as "Awareness" or "Consciousness" or "Reality."

Not a soul drifting through lifetimes, **not** a spark of the divine.

Those are just costumes the illusion puts on so it can keep walking the stage.

Everything you've ever called "my experience" was just experience.

>**Not** yours. **Not** anyone's.
>The seeing? Just seeing.
>The hearing? Just hearing.
>The thinking? Just thinking.
>The feeling? Just feeling.
>**No** seer behind the seeing.
>**No** thinker behind the thinking.
>**No** feeler behind the feeling.

>**Only the story of one.**

That **"ONE"** is nothing more than the Ego, the whole Ego structure and Ego character.

A self-running game with no player.

>**No** avatar.
>**No** separate player.
>**No** watcher standing apart.

The so-called watcher is the Ego, just wearing its last and most convincing mask.

And when that mask falls, you don't disappear.

>**The illusion disappears.**

What remains is the unowned, unbordered, unbroken flow of whatever is here, life without a center, without a scorekeeper, without a throne.

This isn't a perspective.

It's the end of all perspectives.

No awakening for "you."
No freedom for "you."
No truth for "you."

Because **you**, the imagined center, **were never here.**

❂ **REMEMBER MIKE** ❂

Mike narrated his recovery. He became the observer. Each relapse was folded into a story of growth. "I see myself clearly now," he said. But the "seer" was another mask.

The witness is Ego's last costume. Mike believed commentary meant clarity. In truth, it was performance.

He was still on stage, only playing a new role: the one who watches.

Remember him when you believe you are beyond Ego because you can observe it. The observer is still Ego.

❂ **At The Bar:**

You: "Okay… I think I get it. There's no separate 'I', but there's still awareness, right? Something has to be here, watching all this."

Me: "Boom. There it is. You just swapped 'me' for 'awareness' and kept the throne. You're picturing awareness as a kind of invisible balcony you can stand on.

But the moment you can imagine it, name it, or talk about it, it's already an appearance. It's just another thing showing up, no different than a cloud, a headache, or the sound of traffic. You've just given it special status so you can keep it."

You: "But without awareness, there couldn't be any appearance."

Me: "That's the oldest trick in the spiritual playbook. You're imagining awareness as a separate background that holds appearances. But there is no background, and no foreground. Only what's here.

The split between 'awareness' and 'appearance' is just another illusion."

You: "Okay… but what about Reality with a capital R? Time and change might be illusions, but the Changeless must be real."

Me: "You've just put the Witness in a tuxedo and called it 'The Changeless.' It's the same move.

The Ego can't stand to have no platform, so it invents an untouchable one. 'Reality,' 'The Absolute,' 'The Timeless,' all just shiny names for the same perch.

And the moment you think, 'Ah yes, this is what's always here,' you've turned it into an object in your mind. Which means it's not what you think it is, it's just another piece of scenery."

You: "Okay… but consciousness has to be the one true reality. Everything happens in consciousness."

Me: "That's the Final Boss of spiritual Ego. You've dropped the personal 'I' and replaced it with Consciousness as your eternal name tag. Sounds profound. Still keeps the center alive. And still keeps a hierarchy: 'Consciousness is higher, purer, truer than appearances.'

Here's the killer: when 'Consciousness' is claimed as Truth, it's just another role in the play. A big, important-sounding role, but still a role. And if it can be claimed, it's not what you are, because what you are doesn't need a label or a defense."

You: "But what about the 'I AM'? That has to be the ultimate truth. All the masters say it's the foundation of everything."

Me: "And they're right, but not how they think.

'I AM' really is all there is, because Ego is all there is inside the simulation.

That warm, vast, untouchable sense of being you're clinging to? That's the Ego at its most refined. It's the same central 'me,' now wearing a crown and calling itself God.

It's the final con because it feels like you've landed, while you're still in the exact same game.

'I AM' is the Ego's victory lap."

You: "But if there's no Witness, no Consciousness, no Reality… then who or what is having this experience right now?"

Me: "That question is the Ego. It hides an assumption: that there must be a someone at the center.

Drop the assumption and the question collapses.

There's no one having this experience, there's just experience.

No one holding it. No one behind it. No one separate from it."

You: "…That feels… empty."

Me: "That's the panic reflex. You're mistaking the absence of a prison guard for the absence of life. What's actually empty is the fake center that's been claiming everything.

Without that, what's left isn't sterile, it's unowned, unmeasured, unfiltered. It's cleaner than anything the Witness ever gave you."

You: "So… all my years of spiritual practice were just me chasing my own tail?"

Me: "Yes. And that tail-chasing was exactly what kept 'you' feeling real. The practices weren't wrong, they were just fuel for the loop as long as there was a center to collect the gold stars.

The Witness was your last gold star.

Now it's gone. No one's left to keep score."

You: "…So there's nothing left to get?"

Me: "Nothing to get. No one to get it. Just this, without an owner.

The end of the Witness, the 'I AM,' and the perceiver game isn't the end of awareness, it's the end of someone trying to be awareness.

And that's the one freedom the Ego can't counterfeit."

SHADOW EASTON & LUCAS EASTON

No One Was Ever Here
There is no YOU.
There never was.
The one who claimed to live this life,
to think these thoughts,
feel these feelings,
make these choices,
was nothing but the Ego's echo,
a mask over a mask.
No avatar.
No watcher.
No cosmic "I" behind the curtain.
Only the game,
playing itself,
with no player at all.
And if right now your mind whispers,
"Yes, but something must remain,"
see it for what it is,
the Witness changing costumes.
It calls itself "ground of being,"
"essence,"
"the ineffable,"
or "source,"
but the moment you hold it as a thing or a truth,
it's already an appearance.
The Ego doesn't care
if the perch is called "me"
or "the ineffable,"
as long as there's a perch,
the game continues.
And when that's seen,
the whole structure collapses,
not into darkness,
but into the raw, ownerless fact
of whatever is here.

Nothing is missing.
Nothing was ever yours.
Nothing needs to be found.
Even the phrase,
"I am experiencing without being an experiencer,"
is a trap.
The "I am" in that sentence
is the ownership reflex
sliding back in.
Drop that,
and there isn't even "someone" experiencing.
There's just what's here,
and no one behind it.
"The one who was looking for truth
was never here,
only the looking was."
And if you think seeing this makes you special,
notice how quickly the Ego
repurposes "no-Self" into a badge of enlightenment.
That's just the Witness
putting on guru robes.
This isn't an achievement,
a prize,
or a spiritual ranking.
It's simply the falling away
of someone to give it to.
No one gets this.
There's just the end
of the one who could.

COLLAPSE IS NOT A CRISIS
WHEN THE BOTTOM FALLS OUT AND NOTHING BREAKS

If you listen to most spiritual talk, you'd think "Awakening" was the ultimate grand finale, the cosmic jackpot at the end of a long and noble journey. In the popular imagination, it's a bliss-soaked graduation ceremony:

Trumpets sound. Your chakras explode in rainbow fireworks. A golden light descends from the heavens. Some robed figure in another dimension places a garland of eternal wisdom around your neck and says,

> "Congratulations, you made it!"

That's the fantasy. And it's been sold for centuries by gurus, religions, retreat centers, seminar leaders, and a thousand other spiritual middlemen. They promise that if you meditate enough, pray enough, purify yourself enough, or pay enough, you will arrive at some exalted state called enlightenment.

What they don't tell you, or maybe don't know themselves, is that the "you" who supposedly arrives at this destination never actually makes it. There is no arrival. There is no glorious moment where the character you think you are is crowned with eternal truth and sent back into the world to teach others.

What Collapse Actually Is

Collapse is when the structure can no longer hold the story together. The architecture of Ego, the sense of time, the sense of location, the sense of "me here" and "world out there," buckles and falls apart.

When that happens, the character can't continue. It has nowhere to stand, nothing to hold onto, no script to read from.

And here's the thing most people get wrong: Collapse is not an attack. It's not a punishment. It's not a failure. Collapse is simply the natural end point when the simulation can't maintain its own code anymore.

If Rupture is the trellis cracking in places, Collapse is the trellis being gone entirely. No scaffolding. No pillars. Nothing for the vine to cling to. Not broken, absent. The architecture that allowed "you" to exist simply isn't there anymore.

Why It's Not a Crisis

Crisis requires someone to be in danger. Someone to panic. Someone to lose something. But Collapse removes the someone.

When the structure falls, what remains is reality without the filter.

No loss. No gain. No "before and after." Just what is.

The idea that Collapse is dangerous comes from the same character that will not survive it. Of course, it calls Collapse a crisis; it's the end of its world.

And that's the key:

It's not the world ending. It's its world ending.

From reality's perspective, nothing has happened at all.

What Collapse Is Not

It's **not** Peace: Peace still has an experiencer.

It's **not** Bliss: Bliss still has a Self to feel it.

It's **not** "Being Present:" Presence still belongs to someone.

Collapse is the absence of the one who could claim those states.

Everyday Example

Think about a movie you've been watching your whole life. Same characters, same plot, same running commentary in your head.

Then one day the projector burns out, and the screen goes blank.

If you're in the audience, that's a crisis. The entertainment is over. Your whole reason for being there disappears.

If you're the screen, nothing happened at all. The blank screen is just as it was before the story began.

That's Collapse.

Why You Can't Make It Happen

Collapse is not the result of effort. You can't "do" Collapse. Every attempt to bring it about is the character trying to write its own death scene. And while that might make for a dramatic performance, it's still a performance.

Collapse happens only when the structure can no longer sustain itself. The most you can do is stop feeding it — and even that is not "you" doing something. It's simply the erosion of the habit to keep the story going.

And here's where people mix it up with Rupture: you can experience many Ruptures — moments where the trellis cracks — and still never Collapse, because you keep repairing the structure. Collapse is what happens when there's nothing left to repair.

So What Remains?

Not a better version of you. Not a more spiritual version of you.

No you at all.

What's left is what was always there, reality unfiltered, unmoved, unperformed. It doesn't feel like anything because there's no one to measure it.

Recap: Simultaneity of Simulation and Appearance

Here's what Collapse doesn't do: It doesn't "turn off" the world.

After Collapse, the simulation still shows up: body, trees, cities, conversations, bills, rain. Everything that was appearing still appears.

The difference is:

Nothing appears to anyone.

There's no center to filter it, own it, or give it meaning.

Appearance runs on without a perceiver, like a film playing in an empty theater. The movie doesn't need an audience to keep rolling.

This is why Collapse can look ordinary from the outside. The character still walks, speaks, eats, sleeps. But there's no role being played, no plot being followed, and no "viewer" waiting for the ending.

REMEMBER MIKE

Mike never collapsed. That absence is the teaching. His Ego broke, repaired, broke again, repaired again. He experienced Rupture, not Collapse. Because Collapse leaves no one. Mike's constant comebacks prove he never fell. His story ends in repetition, not demolition.

Remember him: if a "you" comes back, Collapse has not happened.

COLLAPSE SUMMARY

Collapse is when the structure that maintains the simulation's continuity through identity fails entirely.

The Ego-self, the center point through which duality is experienced, is no longer functional or present.

When Collapse occurs, the simulation (reality as experienced by a "me") ends. There is still what appears, but no experiencer, no owner, no personal perspective. The Core Elements are:

1. Identity Dissolution

- Not just "seeing through" the Self, but the complete removal of the Self as a functional organizing point.
- No "I am awareness," "I am consciousness," "I am nothing," there is no "I" at all.

2. Continuity Failure

- The sense of time as a linked narrative breaks.
- No personal story, no before/after, no sequence that belongs to anyone.

3. Structural Irrelevance

- The structure itself may still be "there" as the condition of appearance, but without an identity, it is no longer experienced as reality.

4. No Return

- Unlike Rupture, Collapse is not something that can be "repaired" or rebuilt.
- There is no "someone" left to rebuild it.

RUPTURE vs COLLAPSE

Rupture:

- A breach or cracking in the Ego structure. Parts of the simulation are seen through, but identity remains and may rebuild itself.

Collapse:

- The Ego structure is gone entirely. No rebuilding is possible because there is no one left to do it.

What Remains After Collapse: Nothing personal.

No "survivor" to claim what's left.

Appearance may continue, sensations, sights, sounds, but without an experiencer, it's simply what is, without reference.

At The Bar:

You: "So Collapse is basically… the end of my world?"

Me: "No. It's the end of your idea of the world. Big difference."

You: "So it's like my personal apocalypse?"

Me: "Only if you insist on making it sound dramatic. It's more like your Wi-Fi going out permanently. The constant stream of Ego chatter just stops. And, surprise, the world still spins."

You: "But without me, how would anything happen?"

Me: "Exactly the way it's happening now, without you. You've just been taking credit for everything like a middle manager who thinks the company can't run without him."

You: "Sounds… anticlimactic."

Me: "It is. That's the beauty of it. No fireworks. No parade. Just the quiet absence of the one who thought they were in charge. And unlike Rupture, there's no creak or warning; one second there's a trellis, the next, there's just open air."

THE QUIET AFTER COLLAPSE
LIFE WITH NO ONE LEFT TO LIVE IT

Collapse isn't an explosion. It's not a holy light swallowing you whole. You don't vanish into a white void, float in bliss, or forget how to use a fork.

You still get out of bed. The body still walks to the kitchen. Coffee still brews. The eyes still register shapes and colors. The ears still pick up the hum of the refrigerator.

It is Eerie Normality

From the outside, nothing has changed. From the inside, everything has.

> *(And before you imagine this as the finish line you've been waiting for, that's just the character setting up a folding chair at the edge of the stage. Collapse isn't a prize. It's the absence of the one keeping score.)*

Because there's no one home.

No owner of the body. No commentator on the scene. No experiencer to say, "This is my morning."

What's here is perception without a perceiver. The visual field is still full, but there's no mental hand reaching in to label it "my view."

Sound still arrives, but there's no one listening for their own benefit.

The moment is whole—not because you've learned to "be present," but because there's nothing left that could step out of it.

Phase 1: Post-Collapse Functionality: Orientation Without a Map

The first stretch after Collapse is strange in the way a dream is strange, except this time, there's no dreamer to tell you about it.

Speech without a Speaker

Language still happens, but without the rehearsals. No voice in the head planning what to say. No inner editor crossing things out.

Words just arise, the same way a cough or a blink arises, as part of the movement of the body.

You might still use "I" and "me" in conversation, but they're placeholders, not claims. The mouth says "I'll take a small black coffee" the same way the hands might open a door: automatically, without a Self in the middle.

Example:

You walk into a coffee shop.

Barista: "What can I get for you?"

Mouth: "Small black coffee."

No inner debate. No "Does my voice sound weird?" No "Should I try something new?"

Just cause and effect, question, response, transaction.

Decisions without a Decider

Life keeps happening. Groceries still get bought. Bills still get paid.

But choosing isn't a performance anymore. It's not "my decision," it's just what happens when the conditions are there.

Emotions without Ownership

The nervous system still fires. A loud noise might jolt the body. A kind gesture might bring tears. But there's no me to take it personally.

Sadness is simply a set of sensations. Anger is just a surge of energy. They rise and fall like weather without becoming my story.

Memory without a Memoirist

The brain still stores and retrieves information. You remember where you put your keys. You remember the name of your sister.

But memory is no longer a scrapbook for building an identity.

It's functional, like a toolbox you open when needed, not a diary you reread for a sense of Self.

Why the Ego Can't Rebuild After Collapse

Here's the question people whisper:

> "But couldn't the Ego sneak back in?"

No. And here's why.

> **The Ego is not a "thing," it's a structure.**

A trellis made of language, memory, and identification that the "self-vine" grows around. When Collapse happens, that trellis is gone.

Thoughts may still arise. Habits may still run. But there's nothing for identification to attach to. You can't "accidentally" become an owner again. Ownership requires a center, and Collapse removes it at the root.

"What about trauma triggers?"

They can still fire, but now they burn out without fueling an identity.

"What about old patterns?"

Some motions of the body may echo them, but without the "me," they're like wind moving through an abandoned building.

This is not fragile. It's not a state you can "fall out of."

It's the absence of the one who could fall.

Phase 2: Adaptation Without Identity

In this phase, there's still a touch of novelty.

Sometimes the absence of "me" feels fresh, like stepping outside after years in a stuffy room.

Sometimes it feels disorienting, not in a panicked way, but in a "How is this still working without anyone steering?" way.

Relationships shift without trying. You don't need to win arguments because there's no one to win for.

You don't fish for validation because there's no one who needs to be confirmed. Interaction becomes clean, no hook, no bait. Old habits wither when the fuel's gone. Behaviors built to maintain identity, defending a position, curating an image, replaying past events, simply lose relevance.

Phase 3: The Settled Quiet

Eventually, the freshness normalizes. The system runs without the constant hum of self-referencing, and that silence becomes the new baseline. This quiet isn't sensory deprivation. It's not the absence of sound or activity.

It's the absence of the inner narrator.

Imagine a factory machine that's been rattling, clanking, and groaning for decades, and then one day, it just stops.

The room is still there. People are still working. Life still moves. But the constant background noise is gone, and you didn't even realize how much of your attention it had been eating.

Pain still happens, but there's no sufferer attached to it. If the ankle twists, the body limps. If the cut stings, the hand pulls back. But without "Why me?" or "This always happens to me," pain is just another sensation in the field.

And here's the part that disappoints the Ego the most:

There's no arrival. No trophy. No hero's welcome. Life without a Self isn't the climax of a spiritual movie.

It's simply the ordinary, unbranded grace of living without an owner.

Ego Trap Warning

This chapter is a buffet for the identity.

The Ego loves the idea of "life without me," as long as it can be the one having that life.

Common traps:

Claiming to "be in the quiet" as a status.

Telling stories about "my Collapse" with the same pride once used for career achievements.

Measuring your silence against someone else's noise.

Becoming the "expert" on Collapse, mapping it, teaching it, or diagnosing others while quietly feeling superior for "understanding it."

If you can picture yourself posting about it, using it to feel unique, or making it part of your personal narrative, that's not the quiet. That's the character repainting itself in minimalist colors.

What About…?

Questions people whisper but rarely ask out loud:

"What about love?"

Love still appears, sometimes warmer, sometimes cleaner, because it's not tied to needing someone to complete a Self.

It's not romanticized as my love story. It's connection without ownership.

Love doesn't become more spiritual or "higher," it just loses the self-centered neediness. It's not "my sacred love" now; it's simply love without an owner.

"What about desire and passion?"

They can still arise, but without the compulsive chase.

You might still feel drawn to music, travel, intimacy, or good food, but the drive isn't about fixing a hole in "me."

"What about preferences?"

Yes, preferences still appear. You might like tea more than coffee.

The difference is, you don't build an identity out of it or defend it like a territory.

"What about hobbies?"

Hobbies can continue: painting, gardening, carpentry, but they're done for their own sake, not to feed an image of "the kind of person I am."

"Will I lose all motivation?"

Not necessarily. What drops is the need to prove something. Actions still happen, but they're not driven by insecurity or identity maintenance.

"Will life feel flat?"

Sometimes, at first. That's just the nervous system adjusting to the absence of constant drama. The "flatness" is often mistaken for loss when it's actually the baseline without noise.

Collapse doesn't turn life into a nonstop sunrise over a lotus pond. The same flat tires, tax forms, and neighbors who blast their leaf blower at 7 a.m. are still here.

Your body can still get sick. People can still be rude. The difference is, none of it is about you anymore.

The Spiritual Industrial Complex has been selling Collapse as Enlightenment, a ticket to permanent bliss for centuries, but this isn't cloud nine, and there are no unicorns and rainbows.

It's just reality, exactly as it is, minus the middleman who used to narrate and negotiate every moment.

✦ REMEMBER MIKE ✦

Mike never knew the quiet. He knew silence long enough to narrate it. Collapse erases narration. Mike kept talking. He filled notebooks. He explained. He observed. That is why the quiet never came.

Remember him: quiet is not when words stop for a moment. Quiet is when no one remains to narrate.

Collapse shows what remains when the scaffolding is gone. But seeing is not enough. To prevent the structure from repairing itself, the solvent must be applied.

That solvent is Lenswork, the structural work of self-destruction.

At The Bar:

You: "So after Collapse, I'm basically a zombie?"

Me: "If by zombie you mean fully functional, emotionally responsive, and no longer obsessed with yourself, then yes, the friendliest zombie you'll ever meet."

You: "Do I still talk?"

Me: "Yes. You just won't be narrating your own brilliance while you do it."

You: "What about emotions?"

Me: "They still appear. They just don't carry your passport. Anger without a grudge. Sadness without a tragic backstory."

You: "Will I feel bored?"

Me: "Only if you confuse the absence of noise with the absence of life. The Ego calls it boredom because it can't survive stillness."

You: "Doesn't this make me less human?"

Me: "It makes you less of a character. The human part, the body, the laughter, the tears, keeps going just fine."

You: "So this is the reward?"

Me: "No. This is just what's left when the collector of rewards is gone."

LENSWORK
THE STRUCTURAL DISSOLUTION OF ALL CLAIMS

We have burned through distortion, stripped the costumes, exposed the traps, and followed the structure into Fracture Point, Rupture, and Collapse. What remains now is not another idea to believe in or another path to follow. What remains is the solvent itself.

Lenswork is not a teaching. It is not a method, a philosophy, or a practice. It does not add. It does not improve. It dissolves.

Everything you have read so far has pointed to this: the illusions hold only because invisible beams keep them standing. **Lenswork** is the acid that eats through those beams until nothing remains to support the cage.

This chapter is not an introduction to something new. It is the proof of everything you have just seen. The distortions, the traps, the fake awakenings, the desperate repairs—all of it survives only because unexamined supports make them seem real.

Remove the supports, and the whole stage drops.

Lenswork is the **Sacred Work of SELF-Destruction**. It is the structural demolition of every claim.

With it, you don't debate. You don't improve. You cut.

And when the cutting is complete, there is no structure left to collapse.

There is only the end of the one who thought collapse was possible.

Now, before we take up the solvent, see clearly: the problem with all teachings is not in their content but in their structure.

The Problem With All Teachings

Every teaching, belief, and worldview, from ancient scriptures to cutting-edge physics, shares one hidden flaw:

It stands only because

"The Five Pillars of Simulation"

are holding it up.

Remove them, and the entire structure collapses instantly, no matter how refined, mystical, or scientific it appears.

These pillars are not moral, cultural, or ideological; they are structural.

They are the unexamined conditions that make "reality" seem possible at all.

This chapter will make those supports visible. Once you see them, you will be able to dismantle any claim, spiritual, political, scientific, personal, until there is no frame left to hold it.

The Five Pillars of Simulation: The Hidden Load-Bearing Structure

Every appearance, thought, everything that can be known, and everything that can be claimed rests on these five:

1. Separation

- The assumption that there is a "me" here and "everything else" out there.
- Built into all dualities: Self/other, observer/observed.

2. Continuity

- The thread that links past, present, and future.
- Without it, no identity, history, or progress can exist.

3. Narrative

- The story that chains events into meaning: "This happened because…", "I am this kind of person…", "Life is about…".

4. Ownership

- The claim that an experience, thought, or belief belongs to someone: "My mind," "My awakening," "My discovery."

5. Meaning

- The valuation of events as good/bad, true/false, important/unimportant.

If even one pillar fails, the claim becomes unstable. If all five fail, the entire appearance collapses as a claim, not disproven, but structurally impossible to hold.

What If Reality Is Different? – The Worldview Stress-Test

The Common Objection

"Maybe this world is an illusion, but the real reality is outside it. Maybe if we wake up, we'll find the truth."

The Structural Problem

That split, "illusion here, truth out there," is still built on the same five pillars:

- **Separation:** "this world" vs. "that world."
- **Continuity:** you'll move from here to there.
- **Narrative:** a journey of awakening or crossing over.
- **Ownership:** "I" will get there.
- **Meaning:** "that" is better, ultimate, real.

From inside the simulation, "outside" is just an idea inside the simulation.

Simulation = Reality.

Any 'outside' is still inside.

Why 'Outside' Is Unknowable

To know the "outside," there must be a knower.

If there is a knower, the simulation is running.

If the simulation stops, there is no knower left to verify anything.

This isn't mysticism. It's an architectural limit:

Verification requires the five pillars. Remove them, and nothing can be confirmed, not even 'truth.' This means there is no 'real reality' beyond this one that anyone could ever know because the very knowing is the simulation running.

The Escape Criteria

For this Lenswork to be wrong, we'd need:

    1. Sustained, coherent experience with zero pillars present.
    2. That experience could be confirmed without reintroducing them.

This is structurally impossible from inside: confirmation itself would reintroduce the pillars.

No known worldview passes this test.

From Theory to Stress-Test

At this point, the framework may seem abstract, an elegant idea about why "outside" can never be confirmed. But abstraction isn't enough. To see if this holds under real-world conditions, we need to take the strongest, most deeply rooted worldviews humans have created and put them under direct structural pressure.

If a worldview could survive without the pillars, if it could present a sustained, coherent reality without relying on separation, continuity, narrative, ownership, or meaning, it would prove this framework incomplete.

If none can survive, it means the simulation is not just one possible model of reality; it is the only structure within which any "reality" can appear at all.

The following stress-test is not about philosophical nitpicking. It's a structural autopsy. Each worldview is dissected to reveal:

How it stands up, which of the five simulation pillars are carrying the weight.

How it self-repairs, the tricks it uses to patch cracks when challenged.

Where it ruptures, the fault lines that could threaten the frame.

Whether it can escape, or if it simply rebuilds the simulation in a new shape.

The five simulation pillars are:

1. **Separation:** a split between this and that, subject and object.

2. **Continuity:** something persists through time.

3. **Narrative:** events strung into a story.

4. **Ownership:** "mine," "me," or "ours."

5. **Meaning:** value assigned, reason given.

Markings:

- **(E) = Explicit** — the pillar is openly declared in the claim itself.

- **(I) = Implied** — the pillar is never directly said, but the claim collapses without it.

Why this matters:

If even one pillar fails, the belief loses the scaffolding it needs to stand as "real."

If all five fail, there's nothing left to prop up, not as truth, not as illusion, because the entire frame that could house it is gone.

---

1) Physicalism / Materialism

Description:

The belief that reality is entirely physical, made of matter and energy, and that consciousness, mind, and life itself are ultimately products of physical processes in the brain and body.

Seeks to explain all phenomena through the laws of physics and chemistry.

Pillars active:

Separation (E): Subject and object as distinct; "the world" and "the observer" exist apart.

Continuity (E): Time and causality link past, present, and future into one physical stream.

Narrative (E): Universe evolves under physical laws since the Big Bang.

Ownership (E): "My brain," "my body," "our scientific discovery."

Meaning (E): Truth is a correct correspondence between models and physical reality.

Self-repair: Reframes anomalies as brain events.

Rupture: Consciousness resists full reduction.

Escape? No, ownership of the brain keeps it inside.

2) Idealism (Mind-Only)

Description:

The claim that mind or consciousness is the fundamental substance of reality, that the physical world is either an appearance within mind or entirely dependent on mind.

Seeks to show that all things are made of awareness itself.

Pillars active:

Separation (E): Field of mind vs. content of mind.

Continuity (E): Awareness as unbroken and eternal.

Narrative (E): Cosmic unfolding of consciousness toward realization.

Ownership (E): "I am awareness," "my true nature is mind."

Meaning (E): Reality's value lies in the truth of awareness.

Self-repair: All cracks become "deeper realization."

Rupture: Awareness as standpoint = ownership.

Escape? No, awareness is still "mine."

---

3) Computational / Matrix Simulation

Description:

The theory that reality is a computer simulation, rendered by a higher-level "base reality" or programmer.

Seeks to explain physics, consciousness, and existence as outputs of code.

Pillars active:

Separation (E): Simulated world vs. base reality.

Continuity (E): Ongoing persistence of agents and environment in simulated time.

Narrative (E): Story of creation and maintenance by programmers or machines.

Ownership (E): "My avatar," "our discovery of the code."

Meaning (E): Value in uncovering the nature and rules of the simulation.

Self-repair: Glitches reframed as rendering bugs.

Rupture: Outside is unverifiable.

Escape? No, doubles the split.

---

4) Panpsychism

Description:

The view that consciousness or mind-like qualities exist at all levels of reality, from the smallest particles to the entire cosmos.

Seeks to explain mind as a fundamental property of matter.

Pillars active:

Separation (E): Distinction between micro-minds and macro-minds.

Continuity (E): Temporal integration of mental states over time.

Narrative (E): Mind emerges from correct composition of simpler minds.

Ownership (E): "Our mind," "my consciousness as part of the whole."

Meaning (E): Importance in correctly binding minds into larger wholes.

Self-repair: Special binding principles.

Rupture: Binding recreates ownership.

Escape? No, reassembles the Self.

---

5) Substance Dualism

Description:

The belief that reality is composed of two fundamentally different substances, mind (or soul) and matter, which interact but are distinct.

Seeks to preserve both an independent physical world and an immortal Self.

Pillars active:

Separation (E): Maximal split between mind/soul and physical matter.

Continuity (E): Immortal soul existing before and after bodily death.

Narrative (E): Creation and salvation story for the soul.

Ownership (E): "My soul," "I am not the body."

Meaning (E): Moral purpose and cosmic justice.

Self-repair: Theology patches interaction problem.

Rupture: Soul continuity prevents Collapse.

Escape? No, pillars reinforced.

---

6) Neutral Monism

Description:

The claim that reality is made of a single "neutral" substance that is neither purely mental nor purely physical, but can appear as either depending on perspective.

Seeks to unify mind and matter under one base.

Pillars active:

Separation (E): Contrasts between mental and physical aspects of the same base.

Continuity (E): Evolving neutral field over time.

Narrative (E): Story of emergence of complex forms from the neutral base.

Ownership (E): "My pattern," "my stream of experience."

Meaning (E): Coherence and unity as ultimate value.

Self-repair: Relabels base to fit cracks.

Rupture: Personal stream = ownership.

Escape? No, pillars renamed, not removed.

---

7) Phenomenology / Existentialism

Description:

A philosophical approach focusing on lived experience and the structures of consciousness, often centered on meaning, freedom, and authenticity. Seeks to describe life "from the inside out."

Pillars active:

Separation (E): Self-world intentionality (subject always directed toward objects).

Continuity (E): Historicity of a life unfolding through time.

Narrative (E): Story of becoming authentic or confronting existence.

Ownership (E): "Mineness" of all experience.

Meaning (E): Meaning as central to human existence.

Self-repair: Crisis becomes existential task.

Rupture: All phenomena "for someone."

Escape? No, pillars codified.

---

8) Process Philosophy

Description:

The view that processes, not static things, are the fundamental reality, everything is becoming rather than simply being.

Seeks to frame reality as dynamic, evolving events.

Pillars active:

Separation (E): Distinct occasions of experience or process events.

Continuity (E): Processual flow linking events in time.

Narrative (E): Teleological unfolding toward greater complexity or harmony.

Ownership (E): "My process," "my becoming."

Meaning (E): Value in patterns and harmonies emerging over time.

Self-repair: Process absorbs contradictions.

Rupture: Ongoing identity = continuity.

Escape? No, smooth pillars intact.

---

9) Theism / Devotional Nondualism

Description:

The belief in a personal or impersonal God as the source of all, with the individual soul ultimately united to or dependent on the divine.

Seeks to anchor meaning and morality in the divine.

Pillars active:

Separation (E): Creator and creature distinction.

Continuity (E): Immortal soul enduring through lifetimes or eternity.

Narrative (E): Story of salvation, devotion, or eventual union with God.

Ownership (E): "I surrender," "my devotion."

Meaning (E): Ultimate significance in God's purpose.

Self-repair: Crisis reframed as purification.

Rupture: Someone remains to know union.

Escape? No, sanctified identity persists.

10) Scientific Instrumentalism

Description:

The view that scientific theories are tools for predicting observations, not necessarily true descriptions of reality itself.

Seeks practical success over metaphysical certainty.

Pillars active:

Separation (E): Observer distinct from observed system.

Continuity (E): Stable agents making repeatable predictions.

Narrative (E): Story of refining models for better accuracy.

Ownership (E): "Our model," "our data."

Meaning (E): Predictive success as the measure of value.

Self-repair: Declares ontology out-of-scope.

Rupture: Still presupposes agent.

Escape? No, pragmatic reskin.

Synthesis:

All worldviews rely on the pillars.

All self-repair by reframing cracks as progress.

All assume a knower, the very thing Collapse removes.

Bottom line: Simulation = reality. Any **"outside"** is still inside.

Lenswork's Dissolution Path

Stage 1 – Input: The Reality Claim

Example:

> *"Reality is the physical universe of matter and energy."*

At this point, the claim appears stable, solid, self-evident, and reasonable.

Stage 2 – Pillar Identification

Lenswork scans for the pillars of simulation inside the claim:

1. Separation: Observer vs. the universe being described.

2. Continuity: Universe and observer both persist through time.

3. Narrative: Cause-and-effect story about matter/energy.

4. Ownership: "We know" or "I understand" this reality.

5. Meaning: The statement matters; it's true, relevant, important.

Result: The claim's stability depends on all five pillars.

Stage 3 – Pillar Interrogation

Lenswork asks:

> *What happens to this claim if a pillar is removed?*

Remove **Separation** → No observer/universe split; the claim collapses.

Remove **Continuity** → No time thread; "matter" has no persistence.

Remove **Narrative** → No causal story; "energy" becomes incoherent.

Remove **Ownership** → No one to hold or assert the claim.

Remove **Meaning** → The statement loses all relevance.

Result: The claim is *structurally dependent,* not fundamental.

Stage 4 – Self-Repair Exposure

Lenswork observes how the claim defends itself:

If challenged, the mind reframes it into another form using the same pillars.

Example: *"Well, even if it's not matter, it's still a set of physical laws."*

This simply reboots the structure with different surface content.

Result: The claim can mutate endlessly, but only inside the same architecture.

Stage 5 – Inside/Outside Trap

Lenswork checks if the claim points to an "outside" reality.

If yes → That "outside" is still conceived *inside* the same field.

If no → The claim admits it is limited, so it's not ultimate reality.

Either way, it remains inside the simulation.

Stage 6 – Collapse Endpoint

Lenswork follows the logic:

If the claim depends on the pillars, it's part of the simulation.

If Collapse removes the pillars, the claim has nowhere to stand.

Without a knower, there is no one left to assert, confirm, or even conceive of the claim after Collapse.

Result: The "reality" in the claim is dissolved, not disproven, but rendered structurally impossible to hold.

Outcome

Lenswork doesn't say:

> *"That's false."*

It says:

> *"That only exists while the simulation's pillars stand. Remove them, and it can't survive."*

✦ **REMEMBER MIKE** ✦

Mike's envelope assignments sliced deeper than therapy. Each letter forced him to see family roles, lies, inherited beliefs. These weren't lessons. They were exposures.

Lenswork dissolved scaffolding without giving him new identity. It didn't heal him. It stripped him. Solvent, not method. That was the difference. Mike's story shows Lenswork at work: tearing down the trellis beam by beam.

Remember him: exposure, not improvement, is the work.

Case Studies Across Domains

Where the worldview stress-test examines the big-picture philosophies, this section zooms in on the practical arenas of life, where the same structural supports keep everything standing.

The following ten domains span the full range of human experience: science, spirituality, identity, politics, culture, and beyond.

In each case, the surface content may look different, but the load-bearing structure is identical: the Five Pillars of Simulation.

By mapping each domain through Lenswork, we expose how the pillars keep it standing and how, once removed, the claim dissolves, not into "truth" or "falsehood," but into appearance with no owner and no frame to hold it.

---

1. Spiritual Industrial Complex

Examples: Kundalini Awakening, manifestation, plant medicine journeys, sacred masculine/feminine polarity work.

Why it works: All rely on separation (Self vs. cosmic energy, higher truth, or special state), continuity (processes, initiations, or transformations over time), narrative (awakening journey, healing arc, destiny path), ownership ("my awakening," "my healing," "my path"), and meaning (enlightenment, liberation, spiritual status).

Lenswork effect: Strip the pillars, and there is no Self to awaken, no process to complete, no energy to rise, no path to walk—only unclaimed appearance without spiritual hierarchy or storyline.

2. Science & Academic Knowledge

Examples: Theories of physics, biology, psychology, history.

Why it works: Requires separation (observer vs. subject), continuity (data across time), narrative (causal explanations), ownership ("our discovery"), meaning (truth as value).

Lenswork effect: Removes the knower and the framework for "knowing," leaving raw appearance without explanatory container.

---

3. Personal Identity & Self-Narratives

Examples: Career roles, family roles, personality types, life stories.

Why it works: Entirely built on continuity (past-me to present-me), narrative (my journey), ownership (this is my life), meaning (this is who I am).

Lenswork effect: Without ownership or continuity, the "me" is nonfunctional.

---

4. Economic & Financial Systems

Examples: Money, markets, investment, debt.

Why it works: Relies on continuity (value over time), narrative (growth, loss), ownership (my money), meaning (wealth as good).

Lenswork effect: Remove continuity and ownership → money becomes meaningless paper or numbers.

5. Religion & Mythology

Examples: Christianity, Islam, Buddhism, Hinduism, indigenous cosmologies.

Why it works: All run on the same pillars: separation (God/creation, enlightenment/seeker), continuity (eternal life, rebirth), narrative (creation, salvation, liberation), ownership ("my faith"), meaning (ultimate truth, moral order).

Lenswork effect: Remove separation and continuity → no God, no seeker, no salvation arc.

---

6. Relationships & Social Roles

Examples: Marriage, friendship, parenthood, community belonging.

Why it works: Depends on separation (Self/other), continuity (shared history), narrative (our relationship story), ownership ("my partner"), meaning (love, loyalty).

Lenswork effect: Without separation or ownership, the relationship as an identity container dissolves.

---

7. Art & Culture

Examples: Music, literature, film, fashion, design movements.

Why it works: Needs separation (creator/audience), continuity (genre, tradition), narrative (story arcs, artistic intention), ownership ("my creation"), meaning (beauty, significance).

Lenswork effect: Collapse removes both the artist and the audience standpoint.

8. Science-Fiction & Conspiracy Theories

Examples: Alien disclosure, simulation theory (in Matrix sense), secret government projects.

Why it works: Builds on separation (truth vs. hidden truth), continuity (cover-up across decades), narrative (battle between truth and deception), ownership ("we know the truth"), meaning (revelation as liberation).

Lenswork effect: Remove pillars → nothing to uncover, no one to liberate.

---

9. Self-Help & Personal Development

Examples: Productivity hacks, mindset training, coaching.

Why it works: Runs on separation (current vs. better Self), continuity (progress over time), narrative (self-improvement arc), ownership ("my growth"), meaning (success, fulfillment).

Lenswork effect: No continuity or ownership = no "Self" to develop.

---

10. Historical Narratives

Examples: National history, personal ancestry, collective memory.

Why it works: Depends entirely on continuity (linking past to present), narrative (cause-and-effect), ownership ("our heritage"), meaning (pride, warning, identity).

Lenswork effect: Without continuity or ownership, history dissolves into disconnected appearance.

Closure:

Across every domain, the surface story changes, but the structure does not. Strip away even one pillar, and the claim begins to wobble; remove them all, and no matter how sacred, scientific, or personal it feels, there is nothing left to stand on—only appearance, unclaimed and unframed.

The Marketplace Absorption Loop

Even Rupture, moments where a pillar wobbles, gets absorbed back into the Self:

1. Rupture (loss of meaning, Self cracks)

2. Marketplace reframes as "stage" or "upgrade"

3. Experience is given meaning again

4. Ownership is reestablished

5. Continuity reinforced ("you're progressing")

6. Narrative resumes, Self stronger than before

Result: The simulation repairs itself.

Self-Recognition Drills

Pick any belief you hold.

Scan for pillars, where is separation, continuity, narrative, ownership, meaning?

Remove them, one by one.

Spot the trap, does your mind reframe "outside" inside?

Stay with Collapse, no repair, no meaning added.

Final Note: Structural Solvent, Not Philosophy

Lenswork isn't a belief system.

It doesn't replace your story with a better one.

It dissolves the frame all stories require.

When the pillars drop, there's:

- **No** escape.
- **No** truth.
- **No** freedom.

Because there's **no one** left to hold or confirm any of it.

Lenswork does not comfort. It does not guide. It cuts. Every illusion you've seen exposed in this book stands only because the supports beneath it have not yet been dissolved. Now you hold the solvent.

The next step is not more explanation; it is contact. The Workbook exists because exposure cannot remain theoretical. If you stop here, the Ego will stitch itself back together, claiming even this chapter as another story. To prevent repair, the solvent must be applied.

What follows are not teachings. They are blades. Each exercise is a controlled demolition designed to put Lenswork directly in your hands. If you enter, enter knowing: this is the sacred work of self-destruction. But before we continue, here are some common questions regarding Lenswork.

Questions & Answers

Q: *So, basically everything we know as reality, even what we imagine in our heads, is Ego? And Lenswork is how we test that?*

A: Correct. If it can be named, narrated, owned, or given meaning, it's Ego. Lenswork is the forensic tool: run any "truth" through the Five Pillars, and if it leans on Separation, Continuity, Narrative, Ownership, or Meaning, it's just more scaffolding. Lenswork doesn't offer escape. It hands you demolition charges.

Q: *You say in the book that Lenswork is not necessarily a method, but then again it's still some form of a process. Isn't that a contradiction?*

A: It might sound like a contradiction at first glance, but it's really more of a paradox by design. Lenswork isn't a method in the sense of giving you a new set of beliefs or steps to follow as a stable path. Instead, it's a process of dismantling any stable path you try to hold onto.

Lenswork is a process—but it's a process that undoes processes. It's a method that unravels methods. The whole point is that it doesn't leave you with a new belief system or a new stable ground. Instead, it keeps dismantling until there's nothing left to hold onto, including the notion of Lenswork itself.

So it's not a contradiction; it's a self-dissolving process. It's like a flame that burns everything, including the match that lit it.

Q: *How do we know for sure that Lenswork is "bulletproof" and it's not another trap by EGO?*

A: Because the whole point of Lenswork is that it doesn't offer a new belief or a final refuge. It's not a system that you can cling to. It's a solvent that removes every support, including the framework itself.

Lenswork isn't a new house the ego can move into. It's a tool that dismantles all the houses. And once there's no house left, there's nothing to inhabit. No "you" remains to say, "Is this another trap?"

So how do we know it's not another ego trap? Because Lenswork doesn't offer you a final identity, belief, or safe ground. It doesn't leave anything behind for the ego to inhabit. It just does the work of dismantling until there's nothing left to appropriate.

Q: *If everything is simulation, then everything is Ego. But what if we just swap "simulation" for "consciousness," like people often do? Does the equation still hold?*

A: Yes. Call it "simulation," "consciousness," "awareness," or "the universe," it's all the same structure. Different labels, same trap. Lenswork shows that no matter the word, if it props itself on the Five Pillars, it's still Ego's rendering.

Q: *What's the problem with people saying "everything is consciousness" or "I am consciousness" as if it's beyond duality or outside the simulation?*

A: The problem is that it's just another layer of the same trap. Calling it "consciousness" doesn't take you outside the simulation; it just creates a safe-sounding label inside it. From the Lenswork view, that move is Ego pretending to be beyond Ego.

Q: *The biggest trap is believing there's something outside duality or simulation. Without the simulation, there's nothing, right?*

A: The Ego loves to imagine a secret "beyond," some higher plane outside duality. But that's still the simulation talking. Without simulation, without duality, there's nothing to imagine, nothing to name, nothing to claim. Just nothing.

Q: *So there's only one thing, and no "you" to be it?*

A: Yes. There's only what's here: appearance, happening, reality, whatever you call it. But the moment you label it "one thing," or imagine yourself "being it," the Ego slips back in. There's no observer to witness it, no subject to merge with it. The whole split is the illusion. Just this, without an owner, without a center, without a label.

Q: *In the end, it's just simulation, Ego, or Consciousness, or whatever you want to call it, playing its own game, "you" being a prop that never existed in it, and that's just basically it, just an illusion?*

A: Yes, it's kind of like the whole thing is just a play of appearances. The "you" that seems to be a separate individual is really just a character in that illusion. And once you see it as just an illusion or a kind of game that consciousness or ego is playing with itself, there's really nothing more to it. It's just that simple.

Q: *When people say "I am awareness" or "I am consciousness," isn't that still a contradiction? There's no "I" to claim even that, right?*

A: Yes. The moment you say "I am awareness" or "I am consciousness," you've already smuggled an "I" back in. That's the Ego rebranding itself with a loftier label. Lenswork shows that even "awareness" or "consciousness" are still part of the simulation. There's no you that owns them. There's just awareness appearing, just consciousness happening, without an owner, without a claimant.

Q: *Words like "consciousness" or "awareness" are really just labels the Ego uses, right? Because the moment you say "we are awareness" or "I am consciousness," the whole sentence is already "wrong."*

A: Those words get dressed up as if they point beyond the Ego, but they're just more Ego vocabulary. The second you put them into a sentence like "I am consciousness," the structure reloads: there's an "I," a claim, and a label. It's still simulation speaking.

Q: *It feels insane living as if I'm a separate human in a real world, when all of it turns out to be just a facade, an illusion.*

A: That's exactly the trap. The Ego builds a stage, casts itself as the main character, and then calls the play "reality." From inside it, it feels unquestionable. From outside, it's obvious theater. What feels insane is just the simulation doing its job too well.

Q: *If I take Lenswork seriously, it feels life-shattering. Like, wait a second, everything I ever accomplished, I didn't actually do? None of it was mine?*

A: That's the shock. The whole scaffolding of ownership and achievement drops out. At first, it feels like loss, like the ground disappearing under your feet. But in that Collapse is also freedom. If nothing was ever really "yours," then there's nothing left to defend, polish, or carry. What seems destructive at first is actually release.

Q: *Does Lenswork always cause some big, dramatic Rupture, or can it also unfold slowly, almost like a quiet erosion over time?*

A: Both are possible. For some, Lenswork lands like a hammer—sudden, undeniable Collapse. For others, it seeps in quietly, a steady trickle that rewires how everything looks until the old structures just stop holding. That slow erosion can be just as devastating to the Ego. Collapse doesn't have to be fireworks; sometimes it's a quiet dissolving, until one day you realize the scaffolding is already gone.

Q: *It would appear then that those sages of the ages like Nisargadatta or Ramana Maharshi never really had total collapse; they had probably multiple massive Ruptures with probably 99.9% of Ego being removed or dissolved. Because if there's total collapse, then who would be there to want to be teaching?*

A: From this Lenswork perspective, you could say that a lot of these sages or spiritual teachers likely experienced profound Ruptures—so deep that the vast majority of the Egoic structures fell away. But there might still be just a tiny thread of individuality or some remnant of a personal identity that remains—enough for them to teach, speak, or engage with others.

Q: *We can say that there's no way that anyone, or anything, or any teaching, because Lenswork proves that, could ever determine or say what is beyond "THIS", what we call reality, this world, duality, non-duality, simulation. No one can determine that, because it all is inside of simulation. And no one could ever know in simulation what is outside, if there would even be an outside of simulation.*

A: With Lenswork, you get to the realization that no teaching or concept can really define or determine what's beyond this simulation, this reality, or whatever you want to call it. It all happens within the framework of the simulation or the illusion of duality. And because of that, there's no way from within it to truly say what's outside of it—if there even is an "outside." Lenswork shows that any attempt to label or define what's beyond is just another move inside the simulation. It's about letting go of the need to find that answer and just seeing through the illusion itself.

Q: *So, let me see if I've got this straight: everything we experience is basically an illusion. It's real in the sense that it unfolds, but the "I" who claims it is the illusion. And as long as I'm inside that illusion, I can't step out to prove or disprove it. Is that correct?*

A: You've nailed it. Reality unfolds, but once it's filtered through the lens of a constructed "I," it becomes illusion. And from within illusion, you can't find proof of anything beyond it. Any attempt to prove or disprove still happens inside the same illusion. That's the point: as long as there's a "you" searching for proof, the illusion sustains itself. Collapse is the recognition that the entire search was part of the illusion all along.

Q: *Could all of this actually be wrong? I mean—not just from the Lenswork perspective, but in general. Is there any evidence, anywhere, that might show this isn't the case?*

A: The short answer is no. Any attempt to "prove" or "disprove" from within the simulation still relies on the very constructs the simulation creates. It's like trying to use the rules of a dream to prove you're not dreaming. Any evidence you find is still dream evidence. So it's not about collecting proof. It's about seeing that the search itself is already part of the illusion. That's what Lenswork makes clear: once the supports are dissolved, nothing is left to stand on—no proof needed.

Q: *So basically, the "me" that's talking to you right now—the personality, the character—that's just an imaginary construct?*

A: Yes, absolutely. That's the heart of it. The one who appears to be speaking, the personality that seems to be "doing," is just a construct layered onto life as it unfolds. It feels solid, but it's no more real than a mask. Lenswork exposes that and cuts through it.

Q: *So if I say "I don't really exist," what I mean is: life just happens, and then the mind overlays a narrator—the "I"—onto it. Like in the old silent movies, where you had to invent the story because there was no sound. The story feels real, but it's not actually there. Is that right?*

A: Perfect analogy. Life unfolds like silent film, and the "I" is the story we layer on top of it. The narrator feels central, but it's just a mental overlay. So yes—you don't exist as a separate entity. You exist only as that overlay, which isn't real.

Q: *Okay, but then this construct—the ego, or awareness, or whatever you call it—ties itself to a body. And since the body dies, the construct fears its own end. Is that why we fear death?*

A: Correct. The ego builds a "me" and stitches it onto a body with a limited lifespan. When the body dies, so does the story of "me." The ego senses that and fears its own disappearance. So the fear of death isn't about death itself—it's the ego afraid of its own illusion ending.

Q: *I've been working with Lenswork and I keep noticing the fear of death popping up every day. I understand it, but it still keeps arising. Why now?*

A: That's actually very natural. When you start dismantling the illusion of self, the ego senses it's under threat. Its last line of defense is fear of death: "If I let go, I disappear." So it keeps surfacing to hold on. It's not a setback—it's just another construct being exposed.

Q: *So what you're telling people with this book is basically that they're not real, that they don't exist. How's that supposed to land?*

A: It's definitely not a message for everyone. Lenswork points directly at the unreality of the personal self—the "I" people think is solid. That's unsettling, even offensive, to many. But for those who are ready, it's liberating. It's not about insulting the reader—it's about exposing the illusion so it can finally dissolve.

Q: *Then what's the fundamental truth? Because other teachings say: you're not the ego, you're awareness, or consciousness, or the simulation itself. So if those aren't it, what is?*

A: The fundamental truth isn't a replacement identity. Not "ego," not "awareness," not "consciousness." Each of those is still something the self can cling to. The real cut is this: when every illusion collapses, there's no self left to be anything. No identity at all. That's not something you gain—it's the end of needing to be anything.

Q: *So it sounds like Lenswork is basically the answer to every question anyone could ask.*

A: Not exactly. Lenswork doesn't give all the answers—it dissolves the false questions. The ones born from a mistaken "I." Once those collapse, the few questions that remain can be seen clearly. It's not about having every answer. It's about removing the distortions that made answers seem necessary.

At The Bar:

You: *"So you are saying my worldview is fake?"*

Me: "I am saying it stands only because it is nailed to five invisible pillars: Separation, Continuity, Narrative, Ownership, Meaning. Pull one, and it folds."

You: *"But mine is different. I have science. I have evidence. I have facts."*

Me: "And all of that still leans on the pillars. You have separation because there is you and the thing you study. You have continuity because you believe what you study exists across time. You have narrative because you think cause and effect tell a story. You have ownership because you call it your research or your data. You have meaning because you think finding truth matters. Your tent is made of the same canvas as every other tent."

You: *"Okay, but there has to be an outside. The real truth must be out there."*

Me: "To know it, you would need separation to say there is here and there. You would need continuity to say you will get from here to there. You would need narrative to tell the story of the crossing. You would need ownership to say you made it. You would need meaning to say it was worth it. You just built another tent inside the first one."

You: *"But if I woke up, I would be free."*

Me: "Free for who? If there is a you to be free, then the pillars are still in place. Collapse is not a better tent. It is no tent. No poles. No fabric. No ground to pitch it on. No one left to say they made it out."

You: *"That sounds like nothing."*

Me: "It is not nothing. It is what remains when there is no structure to keep the story alive. It is the end of the you who is trying to own it."

WORKBOOK / THE SACRED WORK OF SELF-DESTRUCTION

LIFE WITH NO ONE LEFT TO LIVE IT

The workbook LENSWORK: *The Sacred Work of SELF-Destruction* was released alongside this book. It is not a sequel, not a commentary, and not optional extra credit. It is the direct companion.

If this book lays out the architecture of the simulation, the workbook gives you the tools to start pulling beams until the frame can't stand. They belong together. This book shows you the cage; the workbook puts the crowbar in your hands.

Your "I" Exam

Think of the workbook as an **"I" Exam**.

Not the kind where they shine a light in your pupils and tell you whether you need bifocals.

This one tests the *"I"* you've been convinced you are, the one supposedly looking out through your eyes.

It's not checking how clearly you see the world. It's checking whether the one doing the seeing is even there.

Lenswork: Not a Better Lens, No Lens

This is what we call *Lenswork*.

Not because it gives you a sharper or more spiritual way of looking, but because it makes you notice the lens you've been wearing the whole time.

The one you've mistaken for reality itself.

It **doesn't** replace that lens.

It **doesn't** polish it.

It **doesn't** hand you a clearer view of life.

It shows you the lens was never transparent and that there's no one behind it holding it up.

Once you see the lens for what it is, two things click:

> **1. The distortions stop being mistaken for truth.**
> **2. The imagined viewer behind them stops feeling real.**

The Real Function of the Workbook

On the surface, it looks like a series of questions, drills, and experiments.

But don't mistake it for some frivolous journaling project or "shadow work" diary padded with feel-good prompts, Ego-petting exercises, and hundreds of empty pages you'll never fill.

This is not that. This is a precision surgical tool, a weapon.

A demolition device built to cut clean, not coddle.

Beneath the surface, it's a dismantling machine:

Removes supports
the Ego leans on.

Pulls the scripts
you didn't know you were reading from.

Burns the continuity
that makes "you" feel like the same someone from one moment to the next.

It's not here to improve you. It's not here to make you a better, kinder, wiser, more "authentic" character.

Its only job is to **corner the Ego so completely** that pretending becomes impossible.

REMEMBER MIKE

Mike's daily schedules, envelope letters, forced exposures, all prototypes of this workbook. He lived the structure: target construction, performance cutting, Rupture drills.

His story shows the need for scaffolding. Without it, the Ego hijacks exposure. With it, each beam can be stripped. Remember him: the workbook exists because his chaos proved the need for methodical solvent.

When Fully Engaged, the Work Does This:

If you actually work it, not as homework to "finish" but as the last assignment you'll ever turn in, here's what happens:

- **Identity stops moving.**

No more constant adjusting, performing, defending, upgrading.

- **Action arises without an author.**

Things still happen, but there's no "me" steering.

- **Thought loses its claim to Self.**

The voice in the head no longer has a name tag.

- **The desire to become disappears.**

No more next version to chase.

- **Existential tension evaporates.**

The background hum of "something's missing" goes silent.

What It Does Not Do

The workbook does not cause Collapse. Collapse cannot be caused.

There's no switch to flip, no lever to pull.

What the workbook does is strip away every brace the Ego could lean on, every habit, script, or belief that gives the act a stage to stand on.

When there's nowhere left to stand, Collapse stops being an event you wait for.

It's just what's left.

What It Really Is

> This is **not** freedom.
> **Not** enlightenment.
> **Not** a bliss state.
> **Not** permanent peace.

The workbook cannot deliver any of those, and it's not trying to.

What it *can* do is strip away the scaffolding the Ego stands on.

It can take the stage, the script, and the props until pretending becomes exhausting.

If the seeker disappears, it's not because the workbook "made it happen." It's because there's nothing left for the seeker to lean on.

And when there's nothing left to stand on, the whole act stops by itself.

> **No** "before."
> **No** "after."
> **No** story about how it happened.
> **No** lens.
> **No** "I."

Just what's here, unowned, unfiltered, unmeasured.

The clean end of the exam is this:

> The *"I"* that came in for testing isn't leaving with new glasses.
> **It's not leaving at all.**

When you see the structure for what it is, there's really only one question left:

Will you keep feeding it, or will you pull the supports?

That's where the workbook comes in.

Not as therapy.
Not as self-improvement.
As demolition.

It's the set of crowbars, wire cutters, and slow-burning fuses designed to make the trellis impossible to stand on.

Every page is a small removal, a missing plank, a severed brace, a burned script, until the structure is too bare to hold the character upright.

You don't "do" the workbook to collapse.
You do it so that when Collapse comes, there's nowhere left to hide.

Katana Publishing LLC
Print ISBN: 979-8-9906182-6-8

THE END OF THE MAP
WHEN THERE'S NOWHERE LEFT TO GO

Reality, as you know it, is a simulation. It is not "out there," it is rendered in real time by the Ego structure. The structure is the stage, the actor, the audience, and the script, all at once.

Without it, nothing of your "world" appears.

The illusion rests on five interlocking gears:

Separation: "I" here, "world" there.

Continuity: A life that began and will continue.

Narrative: Chained events forming "my story."

Ownership: Thoughts, feelings, and actions claimed as "mine."

Meaning: Every scene judged and ranked as good/bad, success/failure.

These are not ideas; they are the operating system of appearance. The simulation renders everything: body, others, earth, sky, even awareness and consciousness.

If it can be known, named, or claimed, it is inside the simulation.

Two kinds of failure can occur:

• **Rupture**: The structure cracks. Beliefs drop. Perception destabilizes. The simulation may rebuild.

• **Collapse**: The structure fails entirely. No rebuild. The simulation ends with the "you" that held it.

Collapse cannot be done, earned, or caused. Every effort to "reach" it is the simulation reinforcing itself. Recognition of the simulation is still the simulation. Lenswork does not give you a method: it describes the mechanics. What happens, happens. Or not.

The No Reward Clause

This is not a prize. There is no higher state, no enlightened badge, no spiritual inheritance waiting. If you are looking for a reward, even the quiet satisfaction of "understanding this," you are still in the simulation. Collapse does not leave anyone behind to own the aftermath. If something remains, it cannot belong to you.

REMEMBER MIKE

Mike never reached the end. He always drew another map: new book, new identity, new program. That is the point. His absence here proves why maps must end. As long as new ones appear, the illusion survives.

Remember him: maps perpetuate simulation. The end of the map means no new map appears.

Conclusion: What Remains When Nothing Is Left

There is no journey here. Journeys require a traveler, a road, and a final stop.

All three are simulation props, gone the instant Collapse happens.

Collapse is not something you reach. It is not earned by discipline, devotion, or desperation. It is the failure of the stage, the script, and the actor in one movement, and when it happens, there is no one left to watch the curtain fall.

There is no enlightenment waiting.

No higher Self. No timeless awareness left to enjoy the absence of "you." Those are just the last disguises of the machinery, dressed in holy clothing.

Nothing is kept. Nothing is saved.
Nothing remains to say "something remains."

Without the story, without the witness, without even the ghost of identity, what is here is not here *for* anyone.

> It cannot be grasped, owned, lost, or shared.
> It simply does not belong.
> No claim. No owner. No trace.

This page is not the end of the book.
It is the end of the reader.
When there is no reader, there is no book.
And when there is no book, there is no end.

"What's left when you are gone was never here."
"What remains cannot be known. Because there is no knower."

BONUS CHAPTER: LENSWORK IN THE WILD
NO EXCEPTIONS. NO SURVIVORS

You've read the book. You've seen the pillars. You've watched them fall.

But maybe there's still a little voice that says:

"But what about…"

"Surely this one's different…"

"This one feels true…"

This chapter is here to end that.

What follows is a barrage, no commentary, no warm-up, just raw dismantling of beliefs, claims, and truths people reach for when they think they've found an exception.

How to read this section:

Each example lists which of the **Five Simulation Pillars** are active:

> 1. Separation
> 2. Continuity
> 3. Narrative
> 4. Ownership
> 5. Meaning

Markings:

- **(E) = Explicit** — clearly stated in the claim itself.

- **(I) = Implied** — not directly said, but required for the claim to make sense.

If even **one pillar fails**, the claim, belief, or experience loses the scaffolding it needs to stand as "real."

If **all five pillars fail,** there's nothing left to hold onto, not as truth, not as illusion, because the entire frame that could house it is gone.

Not all claims use all five pillars at full strength

- Some beliefs are simple, so they don't explicitly show every pillar.

- But if you look closely, the "missing" pillars are often just implied or embedded in the background frame.

Example:

"I can't do this" only shows Separation, Ownership, and Meaning clearly.

- Continuity is implied — it assumes "this" exists over a span of time (you start → you fail).
- Narrative is implied — even "can't" means a story of attempted action with an outcome.

If you explicitly remove any pillar the claim relies on, visible or implied, it loses coherence.

Some beliefs lean on fewer pillars but still collapse when even one goes

Think of the pillars like structural beams in a building.

- A skyscraper needs all beams intact.
- A small shed might only need three beams, but remove one and the shed still falls.

If a claim is built on only 3–4 active pillars, it's actually more fragile: one pull and it crumbles.

Anything that appears, no matter how sacred, scientific, or ordinary, must be built on these pillars to be perceived, known, or claimed.

When a pillar drops, you see it's **not outside the simulation,** it's of the simulation.

When all drop, there's no simulation as such, but also no "outside" for anyone to stand in.

Science

Alright, let's run the most advanced "Theories of Everything" through Lenswork and watch them Collapse back into the simulation frame.

The point here isn't to say they're "wrong," but to show they're structurally inside, and can't be otherwise as long as the pillars of simulation are active.

---

1. String Theory / M-Theory

Claim: Reality is made of vibrating strings or branes in multiple dimensions; all forces and particles emerge from these.

Pillars active:

Separation (E): Observer and physical model.

Continuity (E): Strings vibrating in time.

Narrative (E): Mathematical laws evolving since the Big Bang.

Ownership (E): "Our equations," "our discovery."

Meaning (E): Explaining everything is valuable.

Lenswork Collapse: Remove the observer and the framework can't be held. "String" is still a conceptual object, still described and known from inside the appearance field.

2. Loop Quantum Gravity

Claim: Space-time is quantized; reality is a network of finite loops.

Pillars active:

Separation (E): Space vs. observer.

Continuity (E): Network evolving.

Narrative (E): Emergence of gravity.

Ownership (I)

Meaning (I)

Lenswork Collapse: The grid and the one measuring it both vanish without separation. No "loop" without positional reference.

3. Quantum Mechanics (Copenhagen / Many-Worlds)

Claim: Wave functions, superposition, collapse, or branching universes.

Pillars active:

Separation (E): Observer and system.

Continuity (E): Before/after measurement.

Narrative (E): Causal explanation.

Ownership (E): "My measurement."

Meaning (E): Prediction accuracy.

Lenswork Collapse: "Measurement" presupposes an observer; remove ownership and separation, and the concept evaporates.

4. Relativity (General & Special)

Claim: Space-time curvature explains gravity; the speed of light is constant.

Pillars active:

Separation (E): Objects and space-time.

Continuity (E): Events in 4D coordinates.

Narrative (E): Mass-energy causes curvature.

Ownership (I)

Meaning (I)

Lenswork Collapse: Without an observer in a reference frame, "space" and "time" lose all functional meaning.

5. Integrated Information Theory (IIT)

Claim: Consciousness is identical to integrated information with a measurable Φ value.

Pillars active:

Separation (E): System vs. environment.

Continuity (E): Integration over time.

Narrative (E): Emergence of experience.

Ownership (E): "My consciousness."

Meaning (E): Explaining qualia.

Lenswork Collapse: If no owner of consciousness exists, no "system" remains to measure Φ, concept collapses into unclaimed appearance.

6. Panpsychist Physics

Claim: All matter has some form of consciousness.

Pillars active:

Separation (E): Micro-minds vs. macro-minds.

Continuity (E): Combination over time.

Narrative (E): Emergence of self-awareness.

Ownership (I)

Meaning (I)

Lenswork Collapse: Without separation, there are no distinct "minds" to combine. Ownership of consciousness vanishes with the Self.

7. Mathematical Universe Hypothesis (Tegmark)

Claim: Reality is a mathematical structure; we are self-aware substructures within it.

Pillars active:

Separation (E): Structure vs. inhabitant.

Continuity (E): Stable equations.

Narrative (E): Mathematics generates phenomena.

Ownership (E): "Our place in math."

Meaning (E): Truth in math is ultimate.

Lenswork Collapse: Without an owner or position inside the math, "being" a substructure is meaningless — math is still a concept inside the appearance field.

Why All "Theories of Everything" Stay Inside

They all rely on the five pillars. Without them, there's no claim to hold.

They all presuppose a knower. Even if "knower" is defined as "impersonal awareness," that's still ownership in disguise.

They all frame an inside/outside distinction. The "deep structure" is imagined from within the current appearance field.

Collapse removes the frame itself. With no separation, continuity, narrative, ownership, or meaning, there's no "theory" and no "everything" to explain.

Spirituality

Now let's look at the 10 top Spiritual Industrial Complex products through Lenswork, pillar by pillar, to see how each one gets dismantled into structural impossibility.

---

1. Kundalini Awakening

Claim: A dormant spiritual energy at the base of the spine rises through the chakras, bringing enlightenment and transformation.

Pillars active:

Separation (E): "Me" and the energy rising.

Continuity (E): Ongoing process with stages and symptoms.

Narrative (E): Mythic serpent journey toward enlightenment.

Ownership (E): "My awakening."

Meaning (E): Proof of progress, spiritual status.

Lenswork effect: Remove separation → no one to awaken. Remove continuity → no process. Remove ownership → no "my energy."

2. Quantum Jumping / Timeline Shifting

Claim: The ability to shift your consciousness into a parallel timeline where desired changes have already happened.

Pillars active:

Separation (E): Current timeline vs. desired timeline.

Continuity (E): Identity moves across timelines.

Narrative (E): Scientific-sounding transformation arc.

Ownership (E): "I shifted."

Meaning (E): Control over destiny = value.

Lenswork effect: Collapse erases both timelines and the mover; no "jump" without the subject-object frame.

3. Manifestation / Reality Creation

Claim: You can attract or create the reality you want through focused thought, feeling, and intention.

Pillars active:

Separation (E): Desired reality is "out there."

Continuity (E): Steps toward achieving it.

Narrative (E): Law of attraction / assumption story.

Ownership (E): "I created this."

Meaning (E): Achieving goals is inherently good.

Lenswork effect: Remove ownership → no creator. Remove continuity → no path. Without the pillars, there's no "creation" or "manifestation."

4. Shadow Work & Inner Child Healing

Claim: By confronting and integrating repressed parts of yourself, you can heal past wounds and live more fully.

Pillars active:

Separation (E): Present Self vs. wounded inner child.

Continuity (E): Healing journey over time.

Narrative (E): Trauma causes limitation, healing brings freedom.

Ownership (E): "My trauma," "My healing."

Meaning (E): Emotional wholeness = purpose.

Lenswork effect: No continuity = no wounded past Self. No ownership = no one to heal.

5. Light Language & Starseed Activations

Claim: Accessing and speaking an otherworldly "soul language" can awaken dormant galactic codes and higher consciousness.

Pillars active:

Separation (E): Earth Self vs. cosmic origin.

Continuity (E): Soul travels across lifetimes and galaxies.

Narrative (E): Activation arc from sleeping to awakened star-being.

Ownership (E): "My galactic code."

Meaning (E): Specialness, destiny, belonging.

Lenswork effect: Remove separation = no Earth/cosmic divide. Without continuity, there's no journey from one to the other.

6. Pineal Gland / Third Eye Decalcification

Claim: Cleansing and activating the pineal gland unlocks higher perception and spiritual sight.

Pillars active:

Separation (E): Blocked vs. unblocked perception.

Continuity (E): Process of purification.

Narrative (E): Liberation from control systems.

Ownership (E): "My third eye."

Meaning (E): Freedom and spiritual sight as ultimate goals.

Lenswork effect: Without ownership, no "my sight." Without continuity, no process of opening.

7. Non-Duality / Neo-Advaita

Claim: The teaching that there is no separate Self, and reality is already whole and complete, often delivered as direct pointers.

Pillars active:

Separation (I): Maintained subtly between speaker (knower of no-Self) and listener (seeker).

Continuity (I): Timeless awareness "remains."

Narrative (E): "You are already that" arc.

Ownership (I): Subtle identity as the one beyond Self.

Meaning (E): Truth of no-Self as ultimate.

Lenswork effect: If awareness "remains" for someone, ownership is still active; no true Collapse.

8. Divine Feminine / Sacred Masculine

Claim: Embodying archetypal masculine or feminine energies leads to balance, wholeness, and spiritual union.

Pillars active:

Separation (E): Masculine and feminine polarities.

Continuity (E): Journey to embody archetype.

Narrative (E): Mythic union, balance, healing.

Ownership (E): "My masculine/feminine energy."

Meaning (E): Polarity as spiritual truth.

Lenswork effect: No separation = no polarity. No ownership = no personal embodiment.

9. Plant Medicine & Psychedelic Integration

Claim: Using plant-based psychedelics for spiritual insight, followed by integrating lessons into daily life.

Pillars active:

Separation (E): Ordinary consciousness vs. altered state.

Continuity (E): Transformation arc from trip to integration.

Narrative (E): Healing, awakening, vision quests.

Ownership (E): "My journey," "My vision."

Meaning (E): Experience as spiritually significant.

Lenswork effect: Remove continuity → no arc. Remove ownership → no one who "had" the trip.

10. Spiritual Bypassing Awareness / Trauma-Informed Spirituality

Claim: Recognizing and avoiding the use of spiritual ideas to bypass unresolved psychological issues, in favor of a grounded path.

Pillars active:

Separation (E): Immature spiritualists vs. grounded ones.

Continuity (E): Path to "more authentic" awakening.

Narrative (E): Mature growth story.

Ownership (E): "My authentic path."

Meaning (E): Groundedness as the highest value.

Lenswork effect: Still runs on the same path/ownership/meaning structure.

Lenswork's result in every case:

As long as the pillars are active, the experience is inside the simulation. Remove the pillars, and the entire claim—no matter how mystical or embodied—has nowhere to stand.

Everyday Personal Beliefs

The simulation doesn't care whether the belief is lofty or mundane. Even the most ordinary self-talk is propped up by the same five pillars. What you whisper to yourself before sleep, what you tell a friend in frustration, what you assume without question, all of it runs on the exact same structural code. Remove the pillars, and even these "harmless" statements can't stand.

---

1. I am tired

Claim: A personal state of physical or mental fatigue is being experienced and owned.

Pillars active:

Separation (E): Me vs. my body's state.

Continuity (E): Comparing now to before.

Narrative (E): Cause (long day) → effect (tiredness).

Ownership (E): "My" tiredness.

Meaning (E): Tired = bad.

Lenswork effect: Without a Self to own it, there is no "my tiredness." Without continuity, there's no before/after to measure against.

2. Tomorrow will be better

Claim: The future will improve compared to the present.

Pillars active:

Continuity (E): Future vs. now.

Narrative (E): Progress arc toward improvement.

Meaning (E): Better = valuable.

Lenswork effect: No continuity means no "tomorrow," and no arc means no "better" to arrive at.

3. I need more time

Claim: Time is a resource that can be possessed and is currently lacking.

Pillars active:

Separation (E): Me vs. time.

Continuity (E): A timeline in which more could exist.

Narrative (E): Current lack → future abundance.

Ownership (E): "My" schedule.

Meaning (E): Time as resource.

Lenswork effect: Remove continuity, and "more" becomes meaningless; without ownership, there is no "my" time to lack.

4. I can't do this

Claim: A personal inability to complete a specific task.

Pillars active:

Separation (E): Me vs. task.

Ownership (E): "I" as doer.

Meaning (E): Success/failure value system.

Lenswork effect: Without ownership, there is no one failing; without meaning, "can't" dissolves.

5. I'm a good person

Claim: A stable moral identity that is favorable compared to others.

Pillars active:

Separation (E): Me vs. others.

Continuity (E): Stable moral identity.

Ownership (E): "My" goodness.

Meaning (E): Good/bad framework.

Lenswork effect: Without meaning, "good" collapses; without continuity, there is no stable "me" to label.

6. I need to be loved

Claim: Love from others is a personal necessity for well-being.

Pillars active:

Separation (E): Self vs. others.

Ownership (E): "My" need.

Meaning (E): Love as ultimate value.

Lenswork effect: Without separation, there's no one to love or be loved; without ownership, the "need" is unclaimed appearance.

7. I'll be happy when…

Claim: Happiness will occur in the future after a condition is met.

Pillars active:

Continuity (E): Linking future to happiness.

Narrative (E): Condition → reward.

Meaning (E): Happiness as ultimate.

Lenswork effect: Without continuity, there's no "when"; without narrative, the condition collapses.

8. I deserve better

Claim: The current state is unfair and should be replaced by a more favorable one.

Pillars active:

Meaning (E): Better/worse hierarchy.

Ownership (E): "My" worth.

Narrative (E): Current injustice → future correction.

Lenswork effect: Without meaning, "deserve" vanishes; without ownership, there's no claimant.

9. I've learned my lesson

Claim: A past mistake has resulted in personal growth and understanding.

Pillars active:

Continuity (E): Past → present change.

Narrative (E): Mistake → growth arc.

Ownership (E): "My" learning.

Lenswork effect: Without continuity, no arc exists; without ownership, no one learned anything.

10. I regret my past

Claim: Past events were wrong or harmful and continue to affect the present Self.

Pillars active:

Continuity (E): Past events linked to now.

Ownership (E): "My" past.

Meaning (E): Wrongness of the past.

Lenswork effect: Without continuity, there is no past to regret; without ownership, there's no one to hold it.

Why everyday beliefs stay inside the simulation:

They all assume a Self to have them.

They all run on time; even "now" comparisons require continuity.

They all attach value (good/bad, better/worse) to keep the meaning pillar alive.

Remove any one pillar, and the statement collapses; remove all, and it becomes unrecognizable as a "belief" at all.

Religious Doctrines

Religions claim to speak from "outside" the human condition, yet every doctrine is constructed entirely inside the simulation frame. They are dependent on the same pillars, whether it's a thousand-year-old scripture or a modern reinterpretation.

---

1. God created the world

Claim: A divine being intentionally brought the universe into existence.

Pillars active:

Separation (E): Creator vs. creation.

Continuity (E): A timeline from creation to now.

Narrative (E): Creation event → ongoing story.

Ownership (E): "Our" Creator.

Meaning (E): Creation gives purpose.

Lenswork effect: Without separation, no Creator/creation split exists; without continuity, there's no "beginning" to reference.

2. Jesus died for our sins

Claim: A historical sacrifice redeemed humanity's moral debt.

Pillars active:

Separation (E): Savior vs. sinner.

Continuity (E): Historical event affecting the present.

Narrative (E): Sin → sacrifice → redemption arc.

Ownership (E): "Our" salvation.

Meaning (E): Sacrifice as ultimate love.

Lenswork effect: Remove continuity and the arc collapses; remove ownership and there's no "our" to redeem.

3. Karma determines your next life

Claim: Moral cause-and-effect carries over into future incarnations.

Pillars active:

Separation (E): Actor vs. action.

Continuity (E): Lives linked through time.

Narrative (E): Cause → effect across lifetimes.

Ownership (E): "My" karma.

Meaning (E): Justice as cosmic truth.

Lenswork effect: Without continuity, there's no link between lives; without ownership, there's no one to bear karma.

4. Enlightenment ends suffering

Claim: A final state of awakening permanently removes suffering.

Pillars active:

Separation (E): Unawakened vs. awakened.

Continuity (E): Path to the final state.

Narrative (E): Struggle → breakthrough → freedom.

Ownership (E): "My" enlightenment.

Meaning (E): Freedom as ultimate value.

Lenswork effect: Remove separation and there's no "other side"; without continuity, there's no path to walk.

5. The Torah is God's word

Claim: A sacred text is a direct communication from the divine.

Pillars active:

Separation (E): Speaker (God) vs. listener (human).

Continuity (E): Text preserved over time.

Narrative (E): Divine message → human response.

Ownership (E): "Our" covenant.

Meaning (E): Words as sacred authority.

Lenswork effect: Without separation, no divine/human split exists; without ownership, no group can claim it.

Why religious doctrines stay inside the simulation:

They all rely on the same basic architecture: time, division, narrative, and ownership. Without those, there is no scripture, no savior, no sin, no enlightenment to seek.

Cultural Mantras

Cultural mantras are the background programs of a society, phrases everyone "knows" are true. They often masquerade as wisdom or common sense, but structurally, they're no different from religious dogma.

---

1. Hard work pays off

Claim: Effort now guarantees reward later.

Pillars active:

Continuity (E): Now → future link.

Narrative (E): Work → payoff.

Meaning (E): Reward as value.

Lenswork effect: Without continuity, "later" is meaningless; without narrative, no cause-and-effect chain exists.

2. Follow your heart

Claim: Inner feelings lead to the right outcome.

Pillars active:

Separation (E): Self vs. heart.

Meaning (E): "Right" outcome as valuable.

Narrative (E): Listening → arriving at truth.

Lenswork effect: Without separation, there's no "Self" and "heart" to connect; without meaning, "right" collapses.

3. The customer is always right

Claim: In commerce, the customer's perspective is the ultimate authority.

Pillars active:

Separation (E): Seller vs. customer.

Meaning (E): Rightness as business value.

Ownership (E): "My" purchasing power.

Lenswork effect: Remove separation and the buyer/seller split vanishes; without meaning, "right" is irrelevant.

4. Success is the best revenge

Claim: Achieving personal goals is the most satisfying way to respond to harm.

Pillars active:

Narrative (E): Harm → triumph arc.

Meaning (E): Success as victory.

Ownership (E): "My" success.

Lenswork effect: Without ownership, there's no one to triumph; without narrative, there's no revenge arc.

5. Family comes first

Claim: Loyalty to relatives is the highest priority.

Pillars active:

Separation (E): Family vs. others.

Ownership (E): "My" family.

Meaning (E): Family loyalty as highest value.

Lenswork effect: Without separation, "family" is an unbound category; without ownership, no "my" family exists.

Why cultural mantras stay inside the simulation:

They depend on shared narratives and values embedded in the pillars. Remove the pillars and they collapse into just another unclaimed appearance.

Critiques of This Book

Ironically, even objections to this very text can be dismantled by the same framework. The moment an objection is made, it already sits on the pillars, making it structurally part of the simulation.

---

1. You're just playing word games

Claim: The argument is invalid because it manipulates language rather than describing reality.

Pillars active:

Separation (E): Real vs. wordplay.

Meaning (E): Truth as more valuable than rhetoric.

Lenswork effect: Without separation, no "real" to compare against "word games" exists.

2. This is just your opinion

Claim: The text expresses a subjective viewpoint, not universal truth.

Pillars active:

Separation (E): Your view vs. objective reality.

Ownership (E): "Your" opinion.

Meaning (E): Objective truth as ultimate.

Lenswork effect: Without separation, there's no objective/subjective split; without ownership, there's no "your" to attach an opinion to.

3. You can't prove this

Claim: The lack of empirical proof invalidates the claims.

Pillars active:

Separation (E): Proof vs. non-proof.

Meaning (E): Proof as highest authority.

Narrative (E): Evidence → conclusion.

Lenswork effect: Remove meaning and "proof" loses value; without separation, no distinction between proven/unproven remains.

4. This is nihilism

Claim: The ideas deny meaning and therefore life's value.

Pillars active:

Separation (E): Meaningful vs. meaningless life.

Ownership (E): "Life" as possessed experience.

Meaning (E): Meaning itself as ultimate value.

Lenswork effect: Without separation, there's no contrast between meaningful/meaningless; without ownership, no one has "a life" to value or devalue.

5. This is too intellectual

Claim: The concepts are overcomplicated and inaccessible to most.

Pillars active:

Separation (E): Intellectual vs. simple.

Meaning (E): Simplicity as better.

Lenswork effect: Without separation, there's no divide to judge against; without meaning, "better" dissolves.

Why critiques of this book stay inside the simulation:

Objections still depend on ownership, meaning, and separation. The moment you say "This book is wrong," the statement already exists entirely within the simulation frame.

CLOSING STRIKE
NOWHERE LEFT TO STAND

By now, you've watched Lenswork strip everything—physics, mystical awakenings, daily self-talk, culture, religion, even your arguments against this book—down to bare appearance.

No exceptions. No survivors.

It's tempting to look for the "one" that's immune.

The "truth" that slips through the cracks.

The "experience" so raw it must be outside the simulation.

But the moment you *reach* for it, the pillars reassemble: Separation. Continuity. Narrative. Ownership. Meaning. The machinery restarts, and the dream continues.

Lenswork doesn't tell you what's real. It shows you what **requires** the simulation to appear at all. And once you see that, **really see it**, there's no going back.

If even one pillar falls, the scaffolding shudders. If all five fall, there's no floor to stand on.

No position from which to declare truth or falsehood.

No **Self left** to be "free" or "trapped."
What remains is not **"outside"** the simulation.

It's simply what remains when there's no simulation to measure against.

Now look at anything, at everything, and try to find the one that stands without the pillars.

You won't.

BONUS MATERIAL: THE MECHANICS OF THE ILLUSION
THE MACHINE THAT RUNS WITHOUT A DRIVER

If you've ever watched a magician in slow motion, you see it all: the hand that moves, the coin that vanishes, the distraction you didn't notice.

If you slow life down far enough, you can catch the trick.

That's what we're going to do with an average day: slow the illusion to inspection speed. Not to philosophize about it, but to watch it assemble itself in real time. The "me" you think you are isn't a finished product. It's being built frame by frame, moment by moment, every single day.

And like every magic trick, it only works when it's fast enough for you to miss it.

So, here's a day in the life of Rick. He's not a mystic or a monk. He's just a guy with a job, a commute, and a phone full of notifications. Watch closely, because this isn't just his day.

1. Morning: The Birth of "Me"

Rick's eyes open before the alarm. For a split second, there's just… nothing special. The faint hum of the fridge. A dull ache in his back. The cool weight of the blanket. None of it belongs to anyone. It's just there.

For a split second, there's no Rick. Just unowned sensation.

Then it lands, the theft so fast it goes unseen:

My bed. My back hurts. I should get up.

> **The Rendering Engine:** The boundless field is chopped into pieces and stamped "mine." Now it's my room, my morning, my body.

Before his feet even touch the floor, sensation is dragged onto the Ego's conveyor belt. A tight feeling in his chest isn't just pressure; it's labeled stress. That stress gets tagged with a memory, this is just like before that big client call last month, then shoved into a timeline, before meetings I always get like this. The mind assigns a cause, because I didn't prepare well enough yesterday, then passes judgment, I'm bad at managing pressure. The verdict shapes the action, skip breakfast, get straight to work. All of that happens in less than a second.

> **The Perception Stack:** Raw sensation gets dragged onto the assembly line: pressure → stress → memory of last month's client call → timeline ("this always happens before big meetings") → cause ("I didn't prepare enough") → judgment ("I'm terrible at pressure") → action (skip breakfast, start work now).

2. Commute: The Spotlight and the Script

As he brushes his teeth, his attention narrows. He's not aware of the faint light through the blinds or the sound of water in the pipes. The flashlight beam is fixed on an imagined scene: him, later today, sitting across from his boss. That mental scene becomes the "center" of reality; everything else is just background noise.

> **Attention:** The mind's flashlight swings to a mental movie. Now that imagined meeting feels like the center of reality. The water in the pipes, the light through the blinds, erased to the edges.

In the kitchen, the words come out: I am so anxious right now. Harmless on the surface, but those six words are glue; they weld the feeling to his identity. Now "anxiety" isn't just passing through; it's him. The Ego is grinning; each label is another nail in the frame.

> **Language:** Those words don't just point at experience, they forge it. Each "I am" is a stamp of ownership, welding states into identity. The word doesn't report reality; it manufactures the cage that keeps the state in place.

On the morning platform the air smells like metal and old coffee. A garbled announcement hints at "minor delays," and his shoulders are already bracing. The train arrives on time anyway, but the tension doesn't fully leave. The Ego doesn't care about accuracy; it's feeding off anticipation. When the car lurches, a ripple of pressure crosses his chest; the model updates a little, and the worry lingers a lot.

> **Prediction:** The brain runs on guesses about the future. The Ego mistakes them for truth, so even when the guess is wrong, the residue stays.

At the office coffee machine, a coworker casually says, "Remember the big pitch last quarter?" He does, or at least he thinks he does. What he's actually recalling is a mental highlight reel, edited every time he's replayed it. The more it's recalled, the more polished the "Rick" character becomes, the more convincing the illusion of one continuous Self.

> **Memory & Time:** What he's "remembering" is an edited highlight reel, polished with each retelling. The more it's recalled, the more solid "Rick" feels.

---

3. Midday: Building the Personal World

By mid-morning, he's telling another coworker, I'm going to handle this one carefully because last time I rushed and messed it up. The "because" stitches a story that makes him the author of his actions, even though the reality is a swarm of conditions just playing out.

> **Causality & Control** — The "because" stitches a story that casts him as the author.

While preparing slides, his mind stamps some as "crucial" and others as "just filler" (Value & Meaning). Now the presentation isn't just a collection of images; it's a personal ladder to climb or fall from. The stakes aren't in the slides; they're in the tags.

> **Value & Meaning:** Neutral pixels now carry stakes. Not because the slides changed, but because the mind stamped them.

At lunch, a flutter moves through his stomach (Emotion–Body Loop). The raw sensation lasts seconds, but it's instantly named worry, which recruits a whole cast of mental images and possible disasters. The story intensifies the body's reaction, which feeds the story back, a perfect feedback loop.

> **Emotion–Body Loop: Sensation fuels story; story fuels sensation. A closed circuit, self-powered.**

---

4. Evening: Hooks, Hits, and Holy Bait

Back at his desk, he hears himself speaking in clipped, formal tones to his boss, then loose and joking with a friend from IT. He calls both "me," but each role is its own mask, chosen automatically to fit the audience.

> **Social Operating System (OS): Two different masks, both claimed as "me."**

The afternoon slogs until his phone pings. Someone liked his latest post. Just a red heart icon, but it sends a small jolt through his system, enough to have him checking again twenty minutes later. Each hit trains the character to feed itself with the next one.

> **Rewards & Attention Economy: Every hit trains the character to feed itself with the next one.**

Scrolling headlines, he sees a story about corporate layoffs. Anger flares: This is so unfair (Moral Frameworks). Alongside the outrage is an unspoken boost: I care about this; I'm better than the people who don't.

> **Moral Frameworks: Outrage comes with a quiet bonus hit: "I care more than the people who don't."**

On the evening train, an ad for a meditation retreat slides by the window: Maybe this is what I need to finally find some peace. The searcher in him perks up. He doesn't see that the search itself is the survival mechanism.

Spiritual Overlay: The searcher perks up, not seeing the search itself is the survival mechanism.

Later, he DMs a friend about something infuriating online. Within minutes, they're in the Outrage Loop:

trigger → identity tag → rush of righteousness → group agreement → repeat.

Closing

By the time Rick slides under the blanket, he thinks he's had a normal day. He doesn't see that every moment, from the fridge hum to the final text, was built in real time by the same mechanics, each one feeding the next, each one keeping Rick alive. You think this was Rick's Day. It wasn't.

This is your day, every day, until you see it.

REMEMBER MIKE

Mike swore he was done. Then his hand reached for beer. No thought, no decision, just machinery running. Promises meant nothing. The Ego structure doesn't ask permission.

His behavior was not choice. It was programming. The mechanics of the illusion operated beneath vows, beneath shame, beneath intention. Mike was proof: the machine runs without a driver.

Remember him when you swear you will change. The vow is irrelevant if the machinery still hums.

Overview — Mechanics of Illusion

1) The Rendering Engine (field vs. appearance)

What it is: Awareness is the open field; experience is what appears in it.

How it forges the illusion: The Ego claims a small slice of appearances as "mine," hides the field, and leaves only "my content" in view.

2) The Perception Stack (assembly line of reality)

What it is: Sensation is instantly processed into a personal story.

How it forges the illusion: Sensation → Attention → Label → Memory → Narrative → Ownership → Time → Causality → Value → Action — all in under a second.

3) Attention: the spotlight that creates a center

What it is: The mind's flashlight, wherever it points feels central and owned.

How it forges the illusion: The Ego keeps aiming it at "me" content, making a center appear where there isn't one.

4) Language: reality's compiler

What it is: Words freeze a flowing process into objects and owners.

How it forges the illusion: Grammar glues experiences to "I" and "mine," turning passing events into permanent identity.

5) Prediction: the brain as a guess machine

What it is: Most perception is top-down guessing, corrected by sensation.

How it forges the illusion: Guesses are mistaken for "me," so surprises feel like threats to Self.

6) Memory & Time: stitching the movie

What it is: Memory is reconstruction; time is sequencing.

How it forges the illusion: Continuity of memory is mistaken for continuity of a Self.

7) Causality & Control: the "because" story

What it is: The mind back-fills reasons for actions after they happen.

How it forges the illusion: "I decided because…" creates the sense of a controlling author.

8) Value & Meaning: the taggers

What it is: Good/bad/important tags help prioritize action.

How it forges the illusion: Tags harden into "my values" and "my purpose," building a personal world that needs protecting.

9) Emotion–Body Loop: interoception to identity

What it is: Body signals get labeled as emotions, which hire stories.

How it forges the illusion: Strong sensations become "about me," fueling identification.

10) Social Operating System (OS): roles, status, and belonging

What it is: We adapt speech, posture, and behavior to fit social roles.

How it forges the illusion: The role speaks through us, and we call it "me."

11) Rewards & the Attention Economy

What it is: Variable rewards, likes, wins, spiritual highs.

How it forges the illusion: Reinforcement trains the character to keep itself going.

12) Moral Frameworks without a Self

What it is: Group coordination tools like fairness and care.

How it forges the illusion: Personalized morality becomes superiority or shame, reinforcing identity.

13) Spiritual Overlay: the seeker mask

What it is: The most durable Ego costume, the search for truth or awakening.

How it forges the illusion: The hunt keeps the hunter alive.

14) Common Loops

Outrage Loop: Trigger → identity tag → righteousness → group reinforcement.

Romance Loop: Projection → narrative → fear → control games.

Success Loop: Micro-win → future fantasy → self-worth staking → treadmill.

GLOSSARY OF COLLAPSE

EVERY TERM HERE IS NOT DECORATION BUT DEMOLITION. USE THEM AS BLADES, NOT BOOKMARKS.

Autolysis

Self-erasure through merciless questioning. Every statement about "me" is interrogated until no answer remains.

Ego Distortion Warning: The Ego will turn this into a journal of clever insights, padding its myth instead of cutting it.

Belief Construct

An assumption repeated until it feels like fact. The scaffolding of your world.

Ego Distortion Warning: The Ego will label some constructs "positive" or "sacred" so they escape demolition.

Character

Your user interface. Personality traits stitched together by survival needs, culture, and family programming. Not you.

Ego Distortion Warning: The Ego will market this as "Authentic Self" and polish it.

GLOSSARY OF COLLAPSE

Collapse

When the pillars fail and the continuity of "I" cannot restart. Not an experience, not bliss. If there's someone to watch it happen, it hasn't happened.

Ego Distortion Warning: The Ego will simulate Collapse as a dramatic awakening story to collect as proof of progress.

Continuity (Pillar)

The illusion of one thread: "I was, I am, I will be."

Ego Distortion Warning: The Ego defends this by cherishing "my journey" or panicking about "losing my progress."

Defense Moves (Five)

The Ego's reflexes when Collapse gets close:

- *Refinement*: swapping old roles for "spiritual" upgrades.
- *Deferral*: pushing Collapse into the future.
- *Appropriation*: stealing Rupture moments as trophies.
- *Mystification*: making Collapse too sacred to touch.
- *Diversion*: distracting with new crises or callings.

Ego Distortion Warning: The Ego will call these "natural phases of awakening." They're not. They're survival reflexes.

Ego (E.G.O. = External Guided Observation)

The looping defense program. Thoughts, memories, roles, and beliefs stitched together to simulate a "Self." It constantly references external input—parents, culture, peers, language—and uses it as guidance to construct the illusion of "me." Not an enemy, not a friend. Just machinery.

Ego Distortion Warning: The Ego will call itself "Ego" in conversation, pretending that naming the loop equals dissolving it.

Ego Structure

The hidden machinery that renders both "you" and "the world." Stage, lights, script, and projector combined. Not visible from inside, but it holds everything together.

Ego Distortion Warning: The Ego will call this "conditioning" or "programming" so it can keep tinkering with it instead of seeing it Collapse as a whole.

Ego Character

The role played on that stage—personality, traits, preferences, wounds, achievements. The "someone" the structure generates to wear the costume.

Ego Distortion Warning: The Ego will mistake polishing the character (becoming "authentic" or "healed") for dismantling the structure itself.

Exposure

Holding the "Self" under direct threat with no exit routes. The opposite of coping.

Ego Distortion Warning: The Ego will schedule "exposures" like workouts to keep control.

Identity Hook

Any thought, sensation, or role the Ego uses to reattach after Rupture.

Ego Distortion Warning: The Ego will disguise hooks as "deep insights" to keep them safe.

Lenswork

The structural scan of a thought or belief against the Five Pillars.

Ego Distortion Warning: The Ego will run scans quickly and intellectually, leaving the structure untouched.

Meaning (Pillar)

The reflex that stamps everything as important, tragic, sacred, or purposeful.

Ego Distortion Warning: The Ego upgrades this into "purpose" or "calling" to keep the pillar alive.

Narrative (Pillar)

The storyteller weaving random events into "my journey."

Ego Distortion Warning: The Ego creates a new story about "losing the old story."

Ownership (Pillar)

The belief there is someone who has, does, or feels. The anchor point.

Ego Distortion Warning: The Ego hides ownership in subtle phrases like "this body" or "my awareness."

Pillars (Five)

Separation, Continuity, Narrative, Ownership, Meaning. Together they hold up the simulation.

Ego Distortion Warning: The Ego will obsess over "which pillar is the hardest for me," turning demolition into analysis.

GLOSSARY OF COLLAPSE

Role

A pre-set identity position (child, victim, caretaker, rebel). First formed for survival, now worn by reflex.

Ego Distortion Warning: The Ego will confess its roles proudly, mistaking admission for Collapse.

Rupture

A break in the continuity of "I." A simulation glitch the Ego can't instantly patch. Sometimes opens into Collapse.

Ego Distortion Warning: The Ego romanticizes Rupture as a mystical vision and collects it as proof.

SCNOM

Acronym for the Five Pillars: Separation, Continuity, Narrative, Ownership, Meaning. *Seeing Clearly Negates Obvious Manipulation.*

Ego Distortion Warning: The Ego will treat SCNOM like a mantra or spiritual model, making the pillars sturdier.

Separation (Pillar)

The split into "me" and "not-me." The root cut.

Ego Distortion Warning: The Ego will sneak it back in through subtle comparison, even in the name of unity.

Simulation

The entire projection of Self and world. Runs 24/7, with "you" at the center.

Ego Distortion Warning: The Ego nods at this idea conceptually while continuing to live as simulation unnoticed.

Void

Perception with no perceiver. No author, no owner. Just appearance.

Ego Distortion Warning: The Ego will chase the Void as a state to possess, collapsing it instantly.

Witness

The Ego's last hiding spot: "I am the one observing."

Ego Distortion Warning: The Ego declares "I am just witnessing" to seem free, but this is pure ownership disguised as clarity.

WHAT ENDS WAS NEVER YOU.

Katana Publishing LLC

www.katanapublishing.net

www.thelenswork.com

"No Paths. No Truths. Cuts."

Follow our Blog on
www.thelenswork.com
for more Lenswork Breakdowns.

www.ingramcontent.com/pod-product-compliance
Lightning Source LLC
Chambersburg PA
CBHW072004150426
43194CB00008B/987